To my grandchildren: Maiya, Lusia, Noble, and Jonah

Trans-Saharan Africa in World History

The
New
Oxford
World
History

Trans-Saharan Africa in World History

Ralph A. Austen

OXFORD

UNIVERSITY PRESS

2010

OXFORD
UNIVERSITY PRESS

Oxford University Press, Inc., publishes works that further
Oxford University's objective of excellence
in research, scholarship, and education.

Oxford   New York
Auckland   Cape Town   Dar es Salaam   Hong Kong   Karachi
Kuala Lumpur   Madrid   Melbourne   Mexico City   Nairobi
New Delhi   Shanghai   Taipei   Toronto

With offices in
Argentina   Austria   Brazil   Chile   Czech Republic   France   Greece
Guatemala   Hungary   Italy   Japan   Poland   Portugal   Singapore
South Korea   Switzerland   Thailand   Turkey   Ukraine   Vietnam

Published by Oxford University Press, Inc.
198 Madison Avenue, New York, NY 10016

www.oup.com

Library of Congress Cataloging-in-Publication Data
Austen, Ralph A.
Trans-Saharan Africa in world history / Ralph A. Austen.
p.   cm.
ISBN 978-0-19-515731-4; 978-0-19-533788-4 (pbk.)
1. Sahara—History.   2. Sahara—Civilization.
3. Trade routes—Sahara—History.   4. Sahara—Commerce—History.
5. Islam—Sahara—History.   I. Title.
DT333.A94 2010   966—dc22   2009034133

3 5 7 9 8 6 4 2

Printed in the United States of America
on acid-free paper

*Frontispiece: A marketplace around the Great Mosque in the Sudanic
West African city of Jenne. This scene embodies the two most important
legacies of trans-Saharan trade: commerce and Islam.*
UNESCO/Alexis N. Vorontzoff

Contents

Editors' Preface

This book is part of the New Oxford World History, an innovative series that offers readers an informed, lively, and up-to-date history of the world and its people that represents a significant change from the "old" world history. Only a few years ago, world history generally amounted to a history of the West—Europe and the United States—with small amounts of information from the rest of the world. Some versions of the "old" world history drew attention to every part of the world *except* Europe and the United States. Readers of that kind of world history could get the impression that somehow the rest of the world was made up of exotic people who had strange customs and spoke difficult languages. Still another kind of "old" world history presented the story of areas or peoples of the world by focusing primarily on the achievements of great civilizations. One learned of great buildings, influential world religions, and mighty rulers but little of ordinary people or more general economic and social patterns. Interactions among the world's peoples were often told from only one perspective.

This series tells world history differently. First, it is comprehensive, covering all countries and regions of the world and investigating the total human experience—even those of so-called peoples without histories living far from the great civilizations. "New" world historians thus share in common an interest in all of human history, even going back millions of years before there were written human records. A few "new" world histories even extend their focus to the entire universe, a "big history" perspective that dramatically shifts the beginning of the story back to the big bang. Some see the "new" global framework of world history today as viewing the world from the vantage point of the Moon, as one scholar put it. We agree. But we also want to take a close-up view, analyzing and reconstructing the significant experiences of all of humanity.

This is not to say that everything that has happened everywhere and in all time periods can be recovered or is worth knowing, but that there is much to be gained by considering both the separate and interrelated stories of different societies and cultures. Making these connections is still another crucial ingredient of the "new" world history.

It emphasizes connectedness and interactions of all kinds—cultural, economic, political, religious, and social—involving peoples, places, and processes. It makes comparisons and finds similarities. Emphasizing both the comparisons and interactions is critical to developing a global framework that can deepen and broaden historical understanding, whether the focus is on a specific country or region or on the whole world.

The rise of the new world history as a discipline comes at an opportune time. The interest in world history in schools and among the general public is vast. We travel to one another's nations, converse and work with people around the world, and are changed by global events. War and peace affect populations worldwide, as do economic conditions and the state of our environment, communications, and health and medicine. The New Oxford World History presents local histories in a global context and gives an overview of world events seen through the eyes of ordinary people. This combination of the local and the global further defines the new world history. Understanding the workings of global and local conditions in the past gives us tools for examining our own world and for envisioning the interconnected future that is in the making.

Bonnie G. Smith
Anand Yang

Preface

This book tells the story of an African world that grew out of more than one thousand years of trans-Saharan trade linking the Mediterranean lands of North Africa with the internal Sudanic grasslands stretching from the Nile River to the Atlantic Ocean. It traces the early role of the Sahara, the globe's largest desert, as a divider that separated these two regions into very different worlds. During the heyday of camel caravan traffic—from the Arab invasions of North Africa in the eighth century CE to the building of European colonial railroads that linked the Sudan with the Atlantic in the early twentieth century—the Sahara became one of the world's great commercial highways. Gold, slaves, and other commodities traveled northward while both manufactured goods and Mediterranean culture moved south. Along with Muslims, North African Jews also played an important role in this commerce.

Over time, cities in the Sudan developed versions of imported handicraft industries and Islamic learning, which they diffused not only throughout their own region and southern forest hinterland but also back across the Sahara. The most enduring impact of this trade and the common cultural reference point of trans-Saharan Africa was Islam. This faith played various roles throughout the region, as a legal system for regulating trade, an inspiration for reformist religious-political movements, and a vehicle of literacy and cosmopolitan knowledge that inspired creativity—often of a very unorthodox kind—within the various ethnolinguistic communities of the region: Arab, Berber, and Sudanic (Mande, Fulani, Hausa, Kanuri, and others).

From the mid-1400s, European voyages to the coast of West and Central Africa provided an alternative international trade route that marginalized trans-Saharan commerce in global terms but stimulated its accelerated local growth. Inland territorial conquest by France and Britain in the 1800s and early 1900s brought more serious disruptions. Trans-Saharan culture, however, not only adapted to these colonial and postcolonial changes but often thrived on them to remain a living force well into the twenty-first century.

Trans-Saharan Africa in World History

CHAPTER I

Introduction to the Sahara: From Desert Barrier to Global Highway

The Sahara desert is a paradoxical place. When most of us hear its name (which means "desert" in Arabic) we picture a vast sea of sand, where very few people could possibly live and where travel is highly dangerous. On maps and in common understandings of geography, the Sahara separates two worlds: the Mediterranean, one of the most dynamic centers of human civilization, and tropical (or "sub-Saharan") Africa, a region often caricatured as "uncivilized."

Yet for more than a thousand years, transportation routes across the Sahara connected the Mediterranean and the rest of the African continent. Camel caravans not only brought highly valued commodities such as gold and slaves to the north but also carried the material goods and culture of Islamic merchants into the desert and across it to the cities of adjoining regions. The Sahara during this era became the center of its own African world, just as traffic on the oceans of the globe created rich, multicultural civilizations around their shores.

Most histories date the beginnings of trans-Saharan trade to some time after the arrival of Islam in North Africa, during the seventh century CE. But the fifth-century BCE Greek author Herodotus describes a trade route from Egypt far into the desert during his own lifetime. When and how did trans-Saharan commerce really commence? Which African peoples, both around and within the desert, were involved in the first stages of this enterprise? What did the new religion and society of Islam add to the impact of earlier civilizations on this region?

Before trying to understand human struggles with the Sahara, we need to look at the geography and natural history of the desert itself. The Sahara is the largest desert in the world, but only 25 percent of its 3.5 million square miles are actually covered by sand. Most of the remaining terrain is almost as dry, however, consisting of gravel and rocky plains and plateaus. The only green portions of this landscape are scattered oases with permanent water and palm trees, as well as

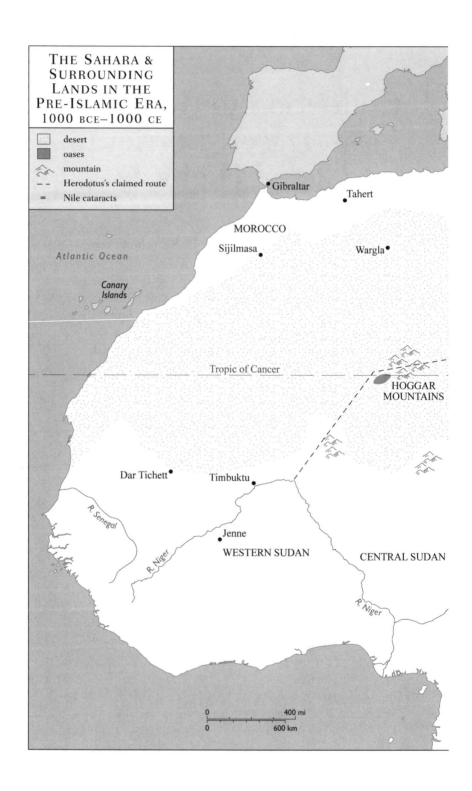

Gibraltar

Tahert

MOROCCO

Sijilmasa

Wargla

Atlantic Ocean

Canary
Islands

Tropic of Cancer

HOGGAR
MOUNTAINS

Dar Tichett

Timbuktu

R. Senegal

Jenne

R. Niger

WESTERN SUDAN

CENTRAL SUDAN

R. Niger

0   400 mi
0   600 km

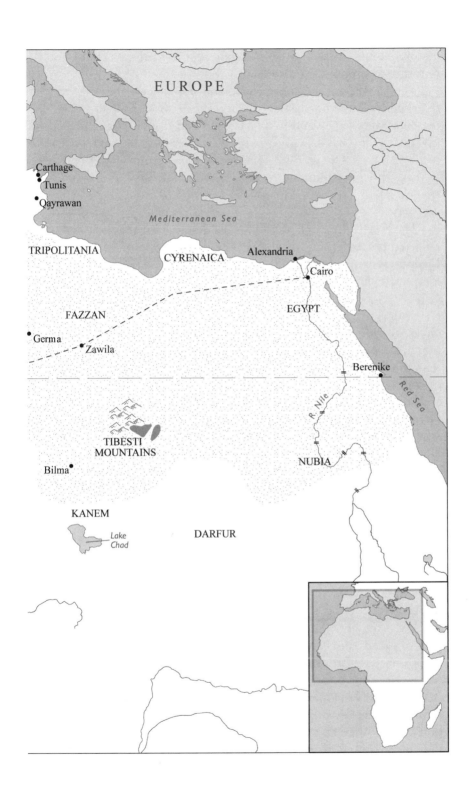

EUROPE

Carthage

Tunis

Qayrawan

Mediterranean Sea

TRIPOLITANIA

CYRENAICA   Alexandria

Cairo

FAZZAN   EGYPT

Germa

Zawila

Berenike

R. Nile

Red Sea

TIBESTI
MOUNTAINS

Bilma

NUBIA

KANEM

Lake
Chad

DARFUR

mountains and other large outcroppings that sometimes capture enough moisture to support vegetation.

The Sahara adjoins more fertile and populated zones of Africa on three sides: to the north, the Mediterranean coastal plain; to the east, the Nile River valley and Red Sea coast; and to the south, the Sudanic savannahs (grasslands).[1] Only in the west does the desert extend directly to the Atlantic Ocean. The conditions for agriculture and commerce in these three surrounding regions are very unequal, and these differences explain a good deal about how the Sahara became a historical highway.

The North African lands above the desert enjoy the same soil types, mild temperatures, and well-distributed rain cycles as the rest of the Mediterranean and most of the northern temperate zone. Indeed "Mediterranean climates," also found at the other end of Africa around the Cape of Good Hope, are among the most favorable in the world for cultivating such staple and luxury crops of the ancient world as wheat, olives, and wine grapes. To the east, Egypt and Nubia (the northern portion of the present-day Republic of Sudan) do not have much more rain than the Sahara. However, the Nile River brings them regular supplies of water and silt (water-borne earth), a gift from the generous rainfall and soils of the East African lands to their south, where the Nile has its origins. Agriculture in the Nile Valley is thus based on the irrigation of a thin but extremely fertile strip of land that is surrounded by desert.

The boundary between desert and cultivated lands at the south of the Sahara is much less clear than in the north, especially in recent decades when the desert has been expanding in this direction. Even within the regions clearly defined as savannah, agriculture is a far more precarious undertaking than on the Mediterranean coast or in the Nile Valley. Rainfall is less plentiful and reliable here and occurs in short seasons that define the time of year when farming is possible. Temperatures in this fully tropical zone also remain quite high, a condition that, in combination with concentrated rainfall, tends to leach nutrients from the ground, leaving very thin topsoil. Wheat, olives, and most fruits will not grow here. Sudanic populations had to develop their own systems of agriculture based on millet and sorghum. These are hardy cereal crops, native to tropical Africa, but they play only a secondary role in temperate zone diets and cannot be exported very far.

As in the Nile Valley, the savannah has a great river, the Niger, which flows from the moist zone of the Guinea highlands through a large portion of the Western and Central Sudan. In some places, especially in the "inner Delta" of central Mali, where the Niger splits into branches and regularly floods the adjacent land, the river's waters also provide the basis for more intensive agriculture, including the growing of native African rice. Before (or at least in a very early stage of) trade across the Sahara, urban centers grew up here and also in the Senegal River valley and around the ancient settlement of Dar Tichett in present-day Mauritania. But even in the most favored of these regions, the possibilities for irrigation from the often sparse Niger waters are limited, as shown by the spectacular failure of the modern Office du Niger. From 1932 to 1984 the French colonial rulers of Mali and their African successors invested millions of dollars in this huge project of dams, canals, and agricultural resettlement, with little or no positive gains. As a result of these difficult agricultural conditions, populations in the Sudanic lands of Africa have always been much sparser than those living directly on the Mediterranean.

Along with a beneficial climate and favorable soil conditions, North Africa and Egypt received great transport advantages from the Mediterranean, a narrow sea touching on three continents. This body of water provided an ideal setting for commerce before the era of mechanized land or air transport, and it is no coincidence that the Mediterranean region became the birthplace of ancient urban civilizations that influenced a much wider world. Egypt enjoyed the advantages of not only Mediterranean contacts but also a second coast to the south. From the third century BCE, ships using the Red Sea port of Berenike could sail directly into the Indian Ocean and establish commercial connections reaching all the way to Southeast Asia.

For internal transportation, Egypt also had the Nile. However, like all African rivers, the Nile is easily navigable only for a limited distance inland, in this case just north of the present-day border with Sudan. Below this line, the flow of water is interrupted by a series of cataracts. Trade between Egypt and Nubia did nevertheless develop as early as 3000 BCE. Water transport was sometimes used for the longer stretches between cataracts, and donkey caravans carried goods along the relatively hospitable landscape near the river and even over short routes through the desert.

Until Europeans sailed to the Atlantic coast of West Africa in the 1400s, the lands to the south of the Sahara had no regular contact with the outside world except via the desert. Even within the Sudan, internal transport is difficult. The Niger River, like the Nile, is blocked by rapids, in this case just as it moves across the present-day border of Niger into the more fertile farmlands of Northern Nigeria. Unlike the Nile, the sources of the Niger do not provide enough rainfall to keep even its flat stretches navigable during all seasons. Land transport in the Sudan is also not easy because in the more southern zones pack animals such as oxen and donkeys fall victim to local diseases, particularly sleeping sickness.

The differences between the ways people lived on either side of the Sahara provide the starting point for the history of trans-Saharan contacts. But the narrative of how these conditions came into being belongs to prehistory, because it occurred in a time for which there are no written accounts or recorded memory. Instead, scholars must rely on evidence from archaeology and geology, which is often difficult to decipher.

One major actor in this narrative is the Sahara itself, which grew and shrank very dramatically in the period immediately preceding its entry into written history. Geologists have established that the desert reached its greatest size around 19,000 BCE, during the Pleistocene epoch (Ice Age), when arid landscapes extended far south into the savannah areas of present-day West and Central Africa. From the end of the Pleistocene period (ca. 9000 BCE) to about 3000 BCE, northern Africa experienced a "wet phase" when greater rainfall shrank the Sahara far below its present size. After 3000 BCE, much drier conditions returned. Although significant smaller-scale climate and landscape shifts continued to take place, by about 300 CE the desert assumed the general proportions we are familiar with today.

These transitions between humidity and aridity played a major role in the human settlement of the Sahara and its surrounding regions. The time of abundant rainfall that preceded 4000 BCE coincides, throughout the Mediterranean world, with the beginning of the Neolithic, or Late Stone Age. During this era, small wandering bands of hunters and gatherers moved into fixed settlements and their populations increased. This new way of life included the addition of clay pottery to stone tools and direct control over food sources. The Sahara was no exception to these changes, although here, as in most of tropical Africa, animal herding and farming occurred only late in the period, mainly as a drier climate began to return. Archaeologists have found evidence of stable communities practicing fishing along with hunting and gathering around the lakes that dotted this region during its early wet phase. Later, when moderate declines in rainfall began to diminish fish and game, people took control over local breeds of cattle and sheep and became herders. The diets of Saharan populations at this time also included some cereals, but it is not clear whether they came from wild or cultivated plants.

Although the Sahara presented few transportation barriers during its wet period, it does not seem that people here established regular contacts with either the Mediterranean coast or the Nile Valley. Saharan populations in this era had neither the motivation nor the means to engage in long-distance trade. Under such favorable climatic conditions, each small community in the region could produce its own basic food, although neighboring groups apparently exchanged some items such as pottery. Movement of goods over wider land expanses would have required animal transportation, and this was not yet available. Saharan peoples did not breed cattle for these purposes, wild donkeys had not been domesticated, and horses reached the region only in the first millennium BCE, when the desert had already returned to a very dry state.

In that later period, Saharan populations became much smaller, and the inhabitants of the scattered oases in the midst of the desert needed goods that had to be brought from distant areas. Rock illustrations made in this time show Saharans using not only draft animals but also wheeled vehicles, so some kind of cross-desert commerce was now possible. But this evidence does not reveal much about the origins and form of such trade.

This rock drawing from the Hoggar Mountains of southwestern Libya indicates that wheeled, horse-drawn vehicles were known in the ancient Sahara. The purpose and extent of this means of travel remains unclear, and it was eventually replaced by the camel. DeA Picture Library/Art Resource

In the southern regions of the Sahara, the drier climate definitely produced new contacts with farming peoples to the south. Some desert communities migrated into better watered areas of the Sudan, such as the inner delta of the Niger River. Here they relied on agriculture for their main food supplies and lived in even more dense settlements than those of the Neolithic Sahara. Settlers in these grasslands suffered from one major limitation. Any cattle kept there throughout the year would fall severely ill during the rainy season, when they were attacked by tsetse flies bearing sleeping-sickness parasites.

This handicap became a stimulus for interdependency between separate communities of farmers and cattle-keepers, involving multiple forms of exchange. Not only could grain be traded for milk products but herds came south from the desert edge during the dry season to graze on already harvested fields. The fields, in return, received the fertilizing benefit of manure deposits. Iron working, which also began in the Sudan during the first millennium BCE, produced further specialization and incentives for regional exchange. As a result of these contacts, urban centers with active regional markets grew up in the savannah regions just south of the Sahara by at least the first century CE.

During its transitions from dry to wet and then to dry again, the Sahara acted like a pump, drawing various populations into it and then sending them back out in somewhat different forms. The resulting distribution of communities around trans-Saharan Africa challenges one of the most powerful and widely-shared beliefs about the division between the northern and southern shores of the desert, that of race.

The earliest written records in North Africa refer to people from the interior of the continent as black: the Greek term "Ethiopian" (also used by Romans and not denoting any specific region of Africa) means "burnt face." The Arabic word for the regions south of the Sahara, Bilad-es-Sudan, translates as Land of the Blacks. The people from other regions of the Mediterranean who made these observations arrived only in the first millennium BCE, well after the Sahara had again become an arid expanse separating the northern half of Africa into two distinct regions. At that time, as now, the native populations of the Mediterranean coast and its immediate hinterland, called Berbers or Libyans, were olive-skinned. Those coming from farther south had much darker complexions, as well as the hair texture and facial features still associated with "black" Africans.

Skeletal remains and Saharan rock paintings from the period of Neolithic settlement, however, show varied racial types inhabiting the same regions. After drier climates returned, Mediterranean Berber-speaking peoples with horses, and later camels, came into the desert and became its dominant population, in terms of both numbers and power. These were the ancestors of the bedouins who continued to control most of the Sahara up to modern times. By the time of the Berber arrival, however, the vast majority of the earlier Saharan population had retreated into more hospitable environments further south. The descendants of these emigrants are now all dark-skinned, but some were clearly of Mediterranean rather than tropical origin.

How much does physical appearance reveal about the larger history of the civilizations that formed in Sudanic West and Central Africa? One theory, long popular among Europeans but also shared by some groups in sub-Saharan Africa, is that peoples from the north—the site of more prosperous and globally linked societies—represent a "superior" race, who subjugated the black "natives" and brought civilization to them. An immediate problem with this view is that the civilization of the Sudan was based on locally developed forms of agriculture. Migrants from the Sahara were almost entirely cattle-herders, who had to adapt themselves to this new environment, often as subjects rather than rulers. The largest of these pastoralist groups, the Fulani or Fula, do claim superiority over the main Sudanic population both because their facial features are somewhat more elongated and thus "white" (i.e., northern) and because they consider cattle-keeping a more noble occupation than farming.

The languages spoken by these groups do not fit well into racial categories. The Fulani or Fulfulde language belongs to the Niger-Congo family, shared by most of sub-Saharan Africa, which includes the Bantu languages that now extend all the way to the Cape of Good Hope. On the other hand, the Hausa, one of the largest Sudanic farming groups with no physical resemblance to Mediterranean peoples, speak a language that belongs to the same Afro-Asiatic family as Berber, ancient Egyptian, Arabic, and Hebrew.

Scholars can only speculate about how these racial and cultural configurations developed. The Fulani probably are descended from populations with a genetic relationship to North Africa whose language changed either in the Sahara or when they migrated to the Sudan. However, there are communities farther east in the Sahara, the Kanuri and Teda, who follow the same pastoral lifestyle as the Fulani yet are linked by both biology and language to the black peoples of the Sudan rather than to the Mediterranean. Ideas about race have been part of the history of trans-Saharan relations, just as they have been in the Atlantic world, but the earliest known movements of peoples in and out of the desert are a caution against using such notions to explain what happened in the more distant past.

Once food-producing communities had firmly settled above and below the Sahara as well as in the Nile Valley, their growth would depend as much on commerce and transport as on animal herding and agriculture. The early towns of Mali, such as Jenne, prospered because their location combined a good food supply with advantageous transport conditions. The proximity of the Sahara encouraged the export of food surpluses in exchange for salt and copper from the desert. Jenne merchants could also use the Niger River and its branches for carrying all these goods as well as iron products for at least medium distances around the desert edge and the savannah.

In the later period of Islamic trans-Saharan trade, the best known city in the Sudan was Timbuktu, located at the northern bend of the Niger. This area is very arid, yet it enjoyed the advantage of being at an intersection of camel caravan routes with the river transport system of the Sudan. The Sudanic peoples had clearly prepared themselves to engage in expanded commerce long before the first caravans ever crossed the desert. But the initiative for such a direct link between the two worlds of Africa would have to come from the more economically advantaged civilizations of the Mediterranean.

The first of these civilizations to establish itself on the borders of the Sahara was Egypt. However, despite their Mediterranean and Red Sea trade, the ancient Egyptians were not themselves great seafarers, nor did they travel much overland into the Sahara. The entire northern African region extending from the Nile Valley to the Atlantic appeared to them as a kind of Wild West (the Arabic name for the region, Maghrib, means "West"), whose desert landscape and nomadic peoples were more a menace than a commercial attraction. The Maghrib first entered the world economy when peoples from outside Africa recognized its strategic position along water routes connecting the eastern Mediterranean with such European sites as Sicily, Sardinia, and Spain.

As early as the ninth century BCE, Phoenician merchants from present-day Lebanon established a major settlement in Carthage (near contemporary Tunis) that soon became the base of a wide maritime empire. In their commerce, the Phoenicians were in constant competition with Greeks, who founded settlements in Cyrenaica (the eastern part of modern Libya) beginning in the eighth century BCE. However, the great political rivals of the Carthaginians were the Romans, who conquered and destroyed the Phoenician outpost in the second century BCE. Rome then established its own extensive North African colonies, dedicated mainly to cultivating wheat and olives for the large urban markets at home.

The hinterland of these foreign settlements, including the northern edge of the Sahara, initially remained under the control of indigenous Berber populations, mainly engaged in herding rather than farming, like earlier Saharan communities. However, the boundaries between the two regions became increasingly porous. On the coast, colonists from outside Africa mixed with and imposed their culture on the main Berber population, who were already settled farmers and sheep-herders. In the interior, Berber chieftains formed kingdoms that engaged in various alliances and rivalries with the Carthaginians and Romans, ultimately forcing the Roman Empire to extend its authority, or at least its influence, well into the desert.

Historians of ancient North Africa are not entirely sure whether relations between its Mediterranean and Saharan regions extended beyond the desert to include trade with the Western and Central Sudan. On balance, available evidence suggests that no significant level of such commerce—or perhaps none at all—took place before the arrival of Arab conquerors in the seventh century CE. But the arguments on the other side—even those with the least foundation—are still worth exploring for what they say about the difficulties of moving beyond the geographical barrier of the post-Neolithic Sahara.

The most romantic claim for such a connection is contained in a sixth century BCE Carthaginian inscription known as "The Periplus [navigation route] of Hanno the Phoenician." This account of a sea voyage to the South Atlantic coast of West Africa includes descriptions of "a land burning full of fragrance" and an island "filled with wild savages. The greatest number of them were females, with hairy bodies, which our interpreters called 'Gorillas.'"[2] Although long taken seriously, this text is now regarded as a Greek literary invention dated at least two hundred years later. Navigators from Carthage did venture beyond the western end of the Mediterranean, but there is no archaeological record of their presence farther south than the Canary Islands or southern Morocco. The sailing technology available at the time would, in any case, have made it impossible to use prevailing Atlantic wind patterns to travel beyond this point and still return home.

A more widespread and contemporary Afrocentric belief concerns the close and long-standing relationship between ancient Egypt and the entire civilization of tropical Africa by way of Nubia in the upper (southern) Nile Valley. From the earliest stages of settled life in this region, close ties existed between Egypt and Nubia involving commerce, politics, and cultural influences in both directions. But there is no indication that towns along the Sudanic portion of the Nile Valley established commercial contacts with regions farther to the west than Darfur (within the present-day Republic of Sudan), nor does archaeological evidence suggest any general Nubian influence in this direction. Even in later periods of extensive long-distance commerce, eastward travel across the wider Sahara from this far south along the Nile was exceptionally difficult and not worth the effort, since the cataracts blocking the river here limited its use for inexpensive transport. Instead, caravans from the Western and Central Sudan, and even from Darfur, made their way north by land to the navigable section of the Nile in southern Egypt or directly to the Mediterranean coast.

During the Carthaginian and Roman periods, some commercial goods did move between the Mediterranean coast of Africa and remote points *within* the Sahara. But the question remains: how active was such trade and how far did it penetrate? Archaeologists have found objects of Mediterranean origin dating to ancient times at various points far south in present-day Libya and Algeria. Here and in portions of southern Morocco, as well as Niger and Mauritania, the dry Saharan climate has also preserved pictures drawn on stone surfaces that depict horse-drawn chariots and ox-driven wagons. These artifacts, which date from Roman times, at least suggest Saharan knowledge of Mediterranean (or contemporary Egyptian) culture and technology.

The illustrations are distributed along two lines of travel that correspond to later caravan trails and have been called "chariot routes." But this name is misleading. It is difficult to imagine how such transportation could have been used for carrying large amounts of goods over long distances in the desert. The Sahara is one of the places in the world where, contrary to the familiar phrase, the wheel had to be disinvented. Horses were used in the desert from early in the first millennium BCE for both warfare and transport, and oxen or donkeys were also employed for carrying goods. But chariots and wagons, especially the kind available in ancient times, do not function well in this difficult terrain. Their representations on Saharan rock surfaces suggests that they were used for fighting, hunting, racing, and ceremonial parades but never for commerce. In fact, we do not even know to what extent wheeled vehicles were present at all in many of the places where their pictures appear. The only certainty is that images of men standing erect in animal-drawn carriages conveyed some kind of prestige, just as such displays did in Roman triumphal processions well after chariots ceased to be employed in actual warfare.

Unfortunately, we cannot learn much about desert trade from Mediterranean writings about North Africa. No records of this kind exist at all for Carthage, since the Carthaginians themselves were very secretive about economic matters and the Romans destroyed every remnant they could find of their bitter enemies. Roman writings on the Sahara mainly describe military campaigns into the desert and depict local populations as, in the words of the first century CE geographer Pliny, "below the level of civilization."[3] On the lands bordering their own settlements and conquered regions in Africa, the Romans erected stone barriers called *limes* that were supposed to keep out the inland "barbarians." (The ethnic name Berber is probably a variant of this negative term, and for that reason some members of this group prefer to be called "Amazigh"; however, the alternate designation has never fully caught on and will not be used here.)

But several centuries before the Romans destroyed Carthage, the Greek historian Herodotus describes what could be a trans-Saharan trade route. It extends from southern Egypt through the Fazzan desert region of modern Libya and into the Hoggar Mountains of southern Algeria, not very far from the Niger Bend. Many modern historians do not take this description very seriously, as Herodotus, referred to as "the father of history" but also as "the father of lies," often reports fantastic and mythological material as if it were fact. However, the route Herodotus traces through the ancient Fazzan is much like one that was well known in later times. Most important, he gives us the earliest literary evidence about a people called the Garamantes, who, between 1000 BCE and 700 CE, created the most elaborate urban society ever to rise in the Sahara.

The richest and most reliable evidence on the Garamantes comes from archeological sources, which reveal that they carried on extensive trade with both Egypt and the Mediterranean coast. However, the key to the Garamantes' prosperity was not commerce but their agriculture, based on a sophisticated system of canal irrigation known as *fogarra*. Roman texts typically tell us only about military conflicts with the Garamantes. Pliny calls them "brigands" who blocked peaceful travel because they "fill up the wells with sand," and for the historian Tacitus, writing in the second century CE, they are "a wild race incessantly occupied in robbing their neighbors."[4]

Beginning around 300 CE the Garamantes did begin to build walls around their towns, suggesting an era of increasing insecurity. It is not clear whether the need for such defensive measures arose from the rising power of camel-riding Berber nomads or conflicts among local farming

Aerial photograph showing the ruins of Germa, the center of the remarkable civilization of the Garamantes in the ancient western Sahara. The Garamantes flourished while the Sahara remained relatively moist, but their cities and agriculture had drastically shrunk by the first century CE. Photo by Toby Savage

populations competing for increasingly scarce sources of water. During this same period of ecological change, fogarra-based irrigation ceased, giving way to reliance on wells. The Garamantes region thus began to resemble other, less densely populated Saharan oasis settlements.

The farming civilization of the Garamantes rose and fell well before the beginning of Islamic-era trans-Saharan trade, and they were more likely its precursors rather than its pioneers. But the account of Herodotus and archaeological discoveries both point toward the spread of the Garamantes' influence in a southwestern direction, so this unique phase of the desert's development does raise important questions about the extent and limitations of commerce within the Sahara during the era of classical antiquity.

Throughout Saharan history, two factors have been critical to long-distance trade: the presence of goods that would bear the cost of arduous desert travel and the availability of transport to make the journeys possible. Mediterranean wares had a wide commercial appeal, and there is no doubt that they found their way into the Sahara in Roman times. However, the archaeology of the Sudanic areas south of the desert, where dense settlement took place before Islamic times, tells a different story. No one has discovered in the Lake Chad area, the Niger Delta, Dar Tichett, or the Senegal River valley enough Mediterranean artifacts dating from before 900 CE to indicate their regular importation. Some historians contend, however, that the two items that dominated exports from the Sudan in Islamic times, gold and slaves, did arrive in the Mediterranean at a much earlier period.

Scholars have found some hints but no solid evidence for a Sudanic gold trade in the era of the Romans and the Byzantines, who succeeded them as rulers of North Africa before the arrival of the Arab conquerors. When the Arabs undertook their first raid into the western Sahara in the eighth century CE, they captured large amounts of gold, so some exports of this valuable metal must have begun before then. However, all the gold that circulated within ancient Egypt and the Maghrib can be ascribed to other sources, including Nubia and, for a brief period, western Morocco.

In the Hoggar Mountains at the very center of the Sahara, archaeologists have excavated a fortress, dated to the fifth century CE, that contains the tomb of a woman known in Berber legend as Princess Tin Hinan. The findings include gold objects of unknown origin and items produced by Romans. Because the Hoggar region is the end point of what Herodotus described as the Garamantes' route into the desert, the contents of Tin Hinan's tomb suggest a possible meeting point of Sudanic gold and Mediterranean manufactures. But no other evidence supports this speculation.

Roman records of trade with the Garamantes mention only one item of high value: "carbuncles," identified by archaeologists as carnelian, a semiprecious stone quarried within the Sahara. The Byzantines, who ruled the Maghrib on the very eve of the Arab conquest, desperately looked for any sources of precious metal connected to this region. But records indicate that the only way they could get gold from their North African provinces was by seizing the plate of local churches.

One of the other things Herodotus tells us about the Garamantes is that they "go in their four-horse chariots chasing the cave-dwelling Ethiopians."[5] This (along with a similar description from a later Roman source) seems to indicate a trade in black slaves, who were certainly present in the Carthaginian, Greek, and Roman worlds. Slaves performed a good deal of the household and agricultural labor in these ancient societies, but the vast majority of the people forced into such work were light-skinned captives (including Berbers) from the many wars and raids these three societies carried out around the Mediterranean. In any case, it is most likely that the enslaved "Ethiopians" described by Herodotus lived within the desert rather than south of it. There have always been black Saharan communities, and horse-drawn vehicles the Garamantes would have used for such raids could not have traveled very far beyond the Fazzan. The victims of these expeditions may well have been the ancestors of the Teda people of Tibesti, a highland desert zone in present-day Chad, which is within reach of the Garamantes' capital. These captives, few as they had to have been, would have sufficed to provide the small black slave population that we know of in the Mediterranean, although the Garamantes probably kept most of them for the intensive needs of their own irrigated agriculture. Thus, as with gold, there is little evidence for a *trans*-Saharan slave trade in ancient times.

The one commodity of Saharan commerce that shows up throughout Herodotus's account is salt. Then, as now, this mineral was found in abundant and convenient form (as large blocks) within the desert and was also in great demand among farming populations of the Sudan. Both people and animals exposed to the hot tropical African climate lose large amounts of body-salt through perspiration. The Sudanic environment provides no sources for replacing this vital substance, except for the very inefficient method of burning local plants to make ash. The urban communities of the Niger Delta almost certainly traded for salt with Saharan peoples, and this commerce might be linked to the route Herodotus traces from the Fazzan. The most likely Sudanic exports, however, were not gold and slaves but agricultural goods and dried fish, for which there would have been demand in the desert but not in the far more distant and fertile Nile Valley or Mediterranean coast.

The transport of salt blocks over extensive tracts within the Sahara required better transport than wheeled vehicles, donkeys, horses, or oxen. The history of any regular long-distance trade across the desert begins only with employment of the camel. Camels can carry heavier loads than horses or donkeys and move faster than oxen. Most important for Saharan travel, they can go long distances without water, thus allowing travel between oases with a minimum of precious cargo weight devoted to provisions instead of commercial goods.

For most of us, the camel is as much part of the Saharan landscape as sand. But even the most "eternal" objects of our imagination have a beginning somewhere in history. Just where this beginning should be situated for North Africa remains a matter of great controversy among historians and archaeologists. The earliest appearance of the camel in the Sahara comes long before anyone believes that trade was carried on across the desert. The wild native African camels whose skeletons were only recently discovered may have largely died out when the Sahara cooled off during the period leading to Neolithic human settlements. Even if they survived, they do not seem to have been herded or used for transport. Therefore, it is most likely that camels themselves, and almost certainly their use as domestic animals, had to be introduced into northern Africa from the Middle East, where such practices became common as early as 3000–2500 BCE. It is of great significance for establishing the origin of trans-Saharan trade to know exactly when camel transport began in the Maghrib, but unfortunately this date remains unclear.

Scholars all agree that the camel did not arrive on the Mediterranean coast of Africa much before the first century BCE. There is less consensus about when camels appeared in Egypt and whether they could have been used on the fifth century BCE Saharan trade routes described by Herodotus. Neither Herodotus nor Egyptian records of this period make any mention of camels, although there is some physical evidence of their presence in the Nile Valley as early as the ninth century BCE. We only get extensive accounts of them during the time when Egypt was ruled by the Ptolemies (a dynasty descended from one of Alexander the Great's generals and ending with Cleopatra), that is, no earlier than 300 BCE. By the first centuries CE, caravans traveling within Egypt and along the North African coast used camels in large numbers, and they were also employed for agricultural labor such as pulling plows and turning water wheels.

Within the Sahara, Berbers took up camels during the same period. They appear on desert rock illustrations dated around 100 BCE, as well as in contemporary Roman accounts of dealings with Saharan nomads, which include references to short-distance north-south caravan trade. The probable source of these animals was Egypt, so it is possible that they carried salt and other goods along the routes Herodotus traces from Egypt into the central Sahara and perhaps even from there to the Niger Bend. Some historians, however, think that the Garamantes took up camels only six centuries later, when they are actually described as using such transport animals, because by then their home region was becoming too dry to support horses.

The bottom line regarding the historical evidence is that before the Arab conquests of the seventh century CE, we have no clear indication of caravan traffic linking the Sudanic and Mediterranean neighbors of the Sahara. What does such silence actually say about this period of Saharan history?

One form of silence that makes the work of historians particularly difficult is the paucity of written records from peoples within or south of the desert. In the Western and Central Sudan, no writing of any kind is known for this period, again suggesting little if any contact with the highly literate Mediterranean. The native populations of North Africa (including the Garamantes) did develop a method of recording their language, inspired by the Phoenician alphabet, which the Tuareg people still use today. Researchers have discovered many inscriptions dating from as far back as the fourth century BCE, but most are grave markers, which contain little historical information. In any case, these documents cannot easily be translated because their ancient "Libyan" language has, at best, a very distant relationship to modern Berber. It is therefore difficult to learn everything we would like to about desert commerce before the arrival of Arabic-speaking merchants. Further archaeological research among the material objects of Saharan and Sudanic society may eventually fill in some of the gaps (as it already has for the Garamantes), but much uncertainty will always remain.

From the more abundant information available about the Romans and Byzantines, it is also evident that the period immediately preceding the Arab conquest was a time of considerable disorder in North Africa. Beginning in the third century CE, the Romans had difficulty defending their frontiers against desert nomads, who gained strength from their acquisition of camels (although the horse remained the main vehicle of local combat). During the same period, Christianity spread rapidly among the populations in the coastal agricultural regions. Instead of inspiring unity, the new faith produced divisions about belief and authority within the Christian church. A group of local priests called Donatists (after their Berber leader, Donatus Magnus) refused to follow bishops appointed by the Roman emperor. This religious dissent helped stir farm workers, slaves, and the general rural Berber population into a revolt against wealthy landowners.

In 429 CE, North Africa was invaded, like many Roman provinces, by a Germanic people, in this case the Vandals of Spain. While not as willfully destructive as their reputation (and the English word derived from their name) suggests, the Vandals were responsible for more than a century of continued warfare as well as renewed conflict between different groups of Christians. In 533, the Romans reconquered North Africa, but not from their historical base in Italy. The new rulers, the Byzantines, were the Greek-speaking successors to the eastern half of the old Roman Empire, with their capital in Constantinople (present-day Istanbul). Far from restoring order to this once prosperous region, Byzantine rule, with its heavy taxes, provoked extensive Berber rebellions, which in turn produced more religious divisions. Scholars know little about what went on in the interior of the Sahara during these centuries of turbulence along the

Mediterranean coast, but it is unlikely that trade with the Sudan could have progressed beyond the direct exchange of desert goods for the products of farmers to the immediate south.

While the introduction of the camel provided the technical means to travel across the entire Sahara, the Carthaginians, the Romans, and their successors evidently failed to establish any social or cultural bonds that extended from the Mediterranean through the desert into the "Lands of the Blacks." That transformation came only with the Arab invasions and the introduction of Islam.

Islam is the youngest of the Mediterranean-based world religions and draws on the traditions of Judaism and Christianity. It originally arose in central Arabia, an environment more akin to Saharan and sub-Saharan Africa than are the worlds of the Mediterranean. Deserts cover much of Arabia, and camels were first domesticated there. The Prophet Muhammad, who founded Islam in the 620s, was a merchant in a newly emerging commercial city. Like most of the other inhabitants of his native Mecca and neighboring Medina, Muhammad was descended from the nomadic tribespeople who still made up the majority population of the Arabian Peninsula.[6] The social content of Muhammad's teachings thus addressed the kinds of conditions that would arise as trade expanded across the Sahara.

The Islamic calendar officially begins in 622, when Muhammad fled from persecution in Mecca to neighboring Medina, where he organized his followers into a strict theocratic state and a powerful military force. After these religious warriors conquered Mecca and the rest of Arabia, Islam expanded northward into Palestine and Syria (Jerusalem is its second most holy city) and then east and west into Iraq and Persia on one side and Egypt on the other. From Egypt, the Arab armies invaded the Maghrib in 643, and Islam entered into the mainstream of trans-Saharan African history.

The Muslim forces that first entered North Africa did anything but restore order to the coastal lands still formally ruled by Byzantium. The earliest decades of these incursions cannot really be described as a time of conquest, since no attempt was made to establish a new system of government. Instead, the invading armies engaged in raids, seizing goods and slaves or, at best, making local communities pay regular tribute. The Arabs also encountered strong resistance from both the Byzantines and indigenous Berbers; one caliph (the successors to Muhammad as head of the Muslim state) is said to have described the regions immediately west of Egypt as "the Gateway to Hell." After they finally drove out the Byzantines, the North African Muslims, who now included more converted and assimilated Berbers than Arabs, still faced repeated political and religious crises. However, even in the extreme turbulence of their earliest presence in the Maghrib, the Muslims directed their energies toward the desert and its southern borders in a way that had little precedent among the previous colonizers of this region.

The first great hero of the Arab conquest, Uqba ibn Nafi, symbolizes this orientation in more senses than one. Uqba is a real historical figure who waged several major campaigns in North Africa between 666 and 683. But most of what is known about him comes from a chronicle written by the historian Ibn Abd al-Hakam centuries later and thus influenced by subsequent events. Like the works of Herodotus, this text contains materials that are difficult to accept as factual. In still later centuries, Berber peoples of the Sahara and even some Sudanic families developed legends about Uqba that use him to link their own communities directly with the Prophet Muhammad. The veneration of Uqba is based on a combination of his known penetration of the Sahara, his brilliant (if probably exaggerated) military feats across North Africa, and his dramatic death at the hands of a great anti-Arab Berber leader, Kusaila.

But the claim that Uqba forced submission on local rulers in the Fazzan and beyond in a 666–67 CE foray does seem to be generally accurate, even if Ibn Abd al-Hakam presents each episode with the same stylized formula: "He seized the king and cut off his finger. The king asked him: 'Why have you done this to me?' Uqba answered: 'As a lesson to you, for when you look at your finger, you won't make war on the Arabs.' Then he imposed on him a tribute of 360 slaves."[7]

Uqba's deepest point of Saharan conquest, a place called Kawar, may be located as far south as the salt-producing center of Bilma in present-day Niger. The scant accounts of Roman ventures among the Garamantes suggest that they reached the same latitudes but in isolated efforts that did not receive much attention or continued support from the imperial bases on the Mediterranean. The story of Uqba, on the other hand, presents us with the glorious beginning of continuing Islamic advances. In the fashion of Arab conquerors in other Mediterranean regions, he also built his capital of Qayrawan ("caravan") as a military encampment in the northern interior of present-day Tunisia, rather than directly on the coast, where the Byzantines still remained.

It would be misleading, however, to say that the Arab leadership sought to exploit the Saharan instead of the Mediterranean resources of North Africa. During the late seventh and early eighth centuries, their energy was devoted mainly to conquering the coastal cities. The crowning achievement of this drive was the invasion of Spain in 711. Yet most of the Muslim forces that crossed over to Europe by this route were Berbers, as was their commander, Tariq ibn Ziyad, for whom Gibraltar is named (Jebel Tariq: "Mountain of Tariq"). Thus for all the conflicts that continued between them, Berber and Arab society were merging into a new Islamic civilization.

The penetration of Islam into the Western and Central Sudan depended on its power to link different groups of people. Yet the first merchants to organize regular trans-Saharan trade were dissident Muslims. During the first century and a half of Islamic presence (650–800), major sectarian and ethnic divisions plagued the Maghrib. The Arab rulers of this period came from a culture that was closer to that of the Berbers than had their Roman, Vandal, and Byzantine predecessors. Like these earlier regimes, however, they imposed heavy taxes on their North African subjects. The terms of submission Uqba imposed on the regions he subdued in the central Sahara included the supply of hundreds of slaves, and this demand continued throughout the region under his successors.

One of the Berbers' responses to such oppression, as in the Christian era, was to embrace unorthodox versions of their new religion. In the case of Islam, that meant Kharijism (from Arabic *kharaj*, "secede"). This version of the faith rejected the authority of the hereditary caliphs who claimed—in Damascus first and later in Baghdad—to be the anointed successors to Muhammad's theocratic rule. The Kharijites were in conflict—often very violent—with the leadership of the core Arab lands in the Middle East, and some of them found refuge and new followers in more marginal areas such as North Africa. Two Kharijite sects set themselves up in different desert-edge regions of the Maghrib during the eighth century: the Ibadis in the hinterland of Tunisia and Algeria and the Sufris in southern Morocco. Both played important roles in establishing caravan routes to the Sudanic lands.

The Ibadis exercised a wider and more enduring influence than the Sufris and left much richer records of their activities. After first challenging the caliph's governor at Qayrawan, the Ibadis formed a large independent state further inland at Tahert in Algeria in 761. In 757 a Berber family of Sufris, the Midraris, created their own smaller state around the newly founded town of Sijilmasa on the Saharan border of Morocco. Until their overthrow in the tenth century, these Kharijite regimes managed to coexist peacefully with the orthodox Muslim regimes nearer the coast. More important, they directed their economic energies toward trans-Saharan enterprise.

The narrative about Uqba ibn Nafi shows that the early Muslim invaders of North Africa were able to advance into the desert but also indicates that they used this capacity to carry on raids rather than peaceful commerce. A Muslim expedition into the Sus region of southern Morocco in 734 even brought back supplies of gold, probably deriving from the Sudan, but there is no evidence of any attempt to follow up this discovery with trading ventures. In fact, orthodox religious authorities considered such commerce with non-Muslim regions undesirable, since Islamic law could not be enforced there. In the tenth century, an Islamic jurist in Qayrawan decreed: "The giving of a *qirad* [money or goods on consignment] which stipulates a journey to the Bilad al-Sudan is not permissible. It is not, in my opinion, like the giving of a qirad for a journey to the cities of Islam."[8]

The Kharijites, as dissident Muslims, were not bound by such prohibitions and, given their inland location, could hardly have chosen not to pursue whatever economic advantages might be gained from the Sahara. Moreover, the leadership of the Ibadi sect did not come from Arabian warrior nobles such as Uqba but from merchant-scholars, often of Persian origin, as were the founders of the Tahert state. Ibadi merchants from Tahert soon spread to the Fazzan, where they entered the (now diminished) Garamantes' capital of Germa but eventually concentrated at Zawila, a trading oasis farther to the south. From here they established commercial links beyond Kawar, the farthest point of penetration by either the Romans or Uqba, into Kanem, the state that dominated the Central Sudan. The main export along this route was slaves, including Berbers from unconquered portions of the Fazzan and now large numbers of black Africans. The key to Ibadi political and economic success in this portion of the Sahara was an alliance with the Mazata, a large Berber tribe who had long fought the Garamantes but now provided camels and guides for extended caravan traffic.

The Tahert regime was destroyed in the early tenth century, but Ibadis continued to dominate the Fazzan for another two hundred years. They also formed a major new settlement at Wargla in southern Algeria, a desert center for the gold trade to the Western Sudan. Here their commercial efforts joined with those of the Sufris, whose capital in Sijilmasa seems to have been an earlier base for this branch of trans-Saharan trade.

The Kharijite settlements in the Sahara provide a recorded beginning point for regular trans-Saharan trade on a significant scale. The combination of economic enterprise and nonaggressive Islamic religious practice that characterized both the Ibadis and the Moroccan Sufris also produced a model for the peaceful linkage of Mediterranean civilization to the Sudanic world. The era of the Sahara as a barrier now ended, and its role as a global highway began.

CHAPTER 2

Caravan Commerce and African Economies

In the year 1324 CE, a memorable event took place in Cairo. Mansa Musa, ruler of the Sudanic empire of Mali, stopped there for three days during a pilgrimage to the Arabian city of Mecca, the spiritual center of Islam. Cairo at this time was an extremely sophisticated metropolis, and its citizens would not ordinarily have paid much attention to foreign travelers. But Mansa Musa was so wealthy and his country so little known to most Egyptians that his expenditures of gold and his conversations with local notables were recorded in great detail. A picture of Mansa Musa decorates the Catalan Atlas of 1375 CE, one of the first sets of European maps to provide serious information about Africa.

The story of Mansa Musa tells a good deal about the role of the Sahara in world history. First, it shows that by the fourteenth century CE the great desert could be safely crossed, even by a mighty king carrying precious goods and accompanied by a large body of followers. Second, it indicates that the lands to the south of the Sahara were now organized into large states and that at least some of their inhabitants had become pious Muslims. Finally, it tells us something about the economic basis for more regular trans-Saharan travel, as Sudanic gold was of great value for both the Islamic world and Christian Europe during the late Middle Ages.

Mansa Musa's pilgrimage took place midway through the great age of camel caravan traffic across the Sahara, which lasted for a little more than a millennium. It began somewhere near the end of the eighth century CE and ended in the early twentieth century, when European-built railroads connected Sudanic Africa to the Atlantic Ocean. Until the late 1400s, when Europeans (still without mechanized transport) first arrived on the coast of West Africa, the Sahara was one of the major trade routes in the world economy. From 1500 to 1900, its global role diminished considerably, but the amount and variety of commerce across the desert actually increased, as did its importance for political, social, and cultural developments within Africa.

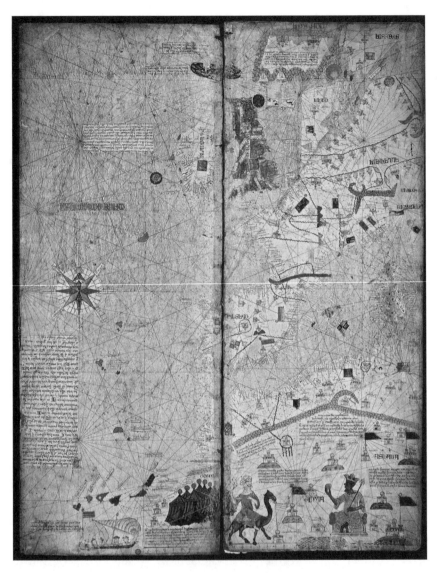

This page and opposite, page from the Catalan Atlas showing many of the principal points of trans-Saharan trade, including, at the lower right, a picture of Mansa Musa, emperor of Mali, holding a gold nugget in his right hand. Abraham Cresques, a Jewish cartographer on the island of Majorca, drew this map in 1375, at a preliminary stage of European sea voyages to West Africa, as indicated by the ship that appears to approach the camel at the extreme lower left. Bibliothèque nationale de France

Those developments were ultimately more significant, at least for Africa, than the trade that made them possible. But the trade itself and its immediate economic aspects came first: What routes did it follow? What goods were carried into and, especially, out of the Sudan? How was merchant movement through the desert organized and who was in control? How were goods for export and for new styles of local consumption produced within the Sudan? Finally, how did all the partners in the trans-Saharan economy respond to the new trading frontier opened by European navigation to Africa's Atlantic coast?

A detailed map of trans-Saharan trade covering the entire history of this commerce would be too cluttered and confusing to read, as the caravans at any one time moved along complex trajectories going not only north and south but also east and west. Not all the caravans traveling through these regions served purely commercial purposes; as in the case of Mansa Musa, they also carried Muslims north and east for purposes of pilgrimage. In addition, the major stopping points and the relative importance of various routes shifted from one period to the next. There is, however, a consistent pattern in the stages of travel: first (if we begin at the Mediterranean) from major coastal cities to intermediary trade centers on the northern Sahara, then across the main desert to the Sudanic trade centers, and finally to the sources of export goods in the Sudan and forest regions farther south. There were oases and highlands in the southern Sahara that served as resting points in the cross-desert trade as well as sources for important goods of their own, such as dates and copper but especially salt.

The most important Mediterranean destinations for trans-Saharan goods stretched along the entire North African coast and included some inland capitals such as Cairo, Tlemcen in Algeria, and Marrakesh and Fez in Morocco. During most periods, Egypt, Libya, and Morocco received more of these caravans than Algeria or Tunisia. In the northern Sahara, some of the oasis towns that had inaugurated cross-desert trade, such as Sijilmasa and Wargla, remained important, but in the Fazzan, Zawila was eventually replaced by the town of Murzuk. A number of new centers arose in the course of the trade, such as Tuwat in the west and Ghat in the south center. Asyut and Jirga on the Nile in southern Egypt served as portals for much of the Cairo-bound traffic.

In the beginning of trans-Saharan commerce, there were two separate Sudanic destinations for caravans. One, on the southern desert edge between Wadan, Timbuktu, and Gao, was focused on gold and connected to towns all across North Africa. The other, seeking slaves from Kanem and its later southward extension, Borno, had links only to the Fazzan. After 1500, however, the cities of Kano and Katsina, founded by the Hausa people of the Central Sudan, became important Sudanic trading centers, and routes connecting them, as well as Kanem-Borno, went northward in all directions. In the 1700s, another exclusively eastward and slave-centered route came into prominence, the notorious Darb-al-Arba'in (Forty-Day Road) from Darfur to southern Egypt.

Like all trading systems, commerce across the Sahara involved goods moving in two directions: from the Mediterranean to the Sudan and from the Sudan back north. However, it is the exports out of sub-Saharan Africa, especially gold, rather than the goods coming in that explain the role of the Sahara in global history. Mediterranean merchants provided Sudanic buyers with the same kinds of commodities they gave the rest of the world: especially cloth but also glassware, armaments, ceramic and metal housewares, paper, horses, and so on. But the Sudan did not buy these commodities in large enough quantities to influence their production in the north.

The goods sent to the Sudan were not only unexceptional but cost very little in Mediterranean markets, in comparison with what came back in return from the south, especially gold. Thus the trans-Saharan trade looks at first glance like a great bargain for the northern merchants. However, when Antonio Malafante, a venturesome Italian of the fifteenth century, thought about entering this market, he was shocked to discover that "the people of Tuat refuse to make any transactions, buying or selling, without a 100 percent commission."[1] Even after it had been well established, the caravan trade clearly remained a risky business that required significant investments of capital. Only Sudanic imports of high value could support such an effort.

Gold remained the most important of the trans-Saharan commodities until the 1500s, when European competition began to draw most of the available gold into Atlantic shipping routes. Even in the earlier centuries, however, large numbers of slaves were sent across the desert, especially from the Sudanic regions east of Mansa Musa's empire, where little gold could be found. After the arrival of European slave traders on the West African and Central African coasts, the trans-Saharan traffic in human beings continued and even increased. In the last five centuries of major desert caravans, the system also proved able to generate significant profits from a greater variety of goods, including goatskins, spices, ivory, gum Arabic, and ostrich feathers.

Historians do not know exactly how much gold flowed across the Sahara between 800 and 1500 CE, but the best estimates put it at a little more than one ton per year. This is very small by comparison with the hundreds of tons produced by modern technology in such places as South Africa. However, medieval mining methods greatly limited the amount of gold that could be obtained anywhere, and the limits of geographical knowledge and transport capacities kept mineral-rich areas of the New World and Australia outside global markets during this era.

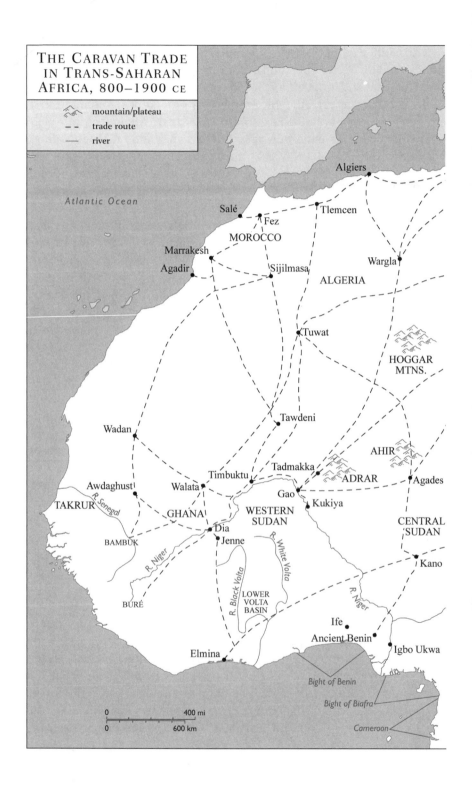

THE CARAVAN TRADE
IN TRANS-SAHARAN
AFRICA, 800–1900 CE

mountain/plateau
trade route
river

Atlantic Ocean

Algiers

Salé
Fez
MOROCCO
Tlemcen

Marrakesh
Agadir
Sijilmasa
Wargla
ALGERIA

Tuwat

HOGGAR
MTNS.

Tawdeni

Wadan

AHIR

Timbuktu
Tadmakka
ADRAR
Agades

Awdaghust
Walata
Gao
Kukiya

TAKRUR
R. Senegal
GHANA
WESTERN
SUDAN
CENTRAL
SUDAN

BAMBUK
Dia
Jenne
R. Niger
R. White Volta
Kano

BURÉ
R. Black Volta
LOWER
VOLTA
BASIN
R. Niger

Ife
Ancient Benin

Elmina
Igbo Ukwa

Bight of Benin

Bight of Biafra

Cameroon

0   400 mi
0   600 km

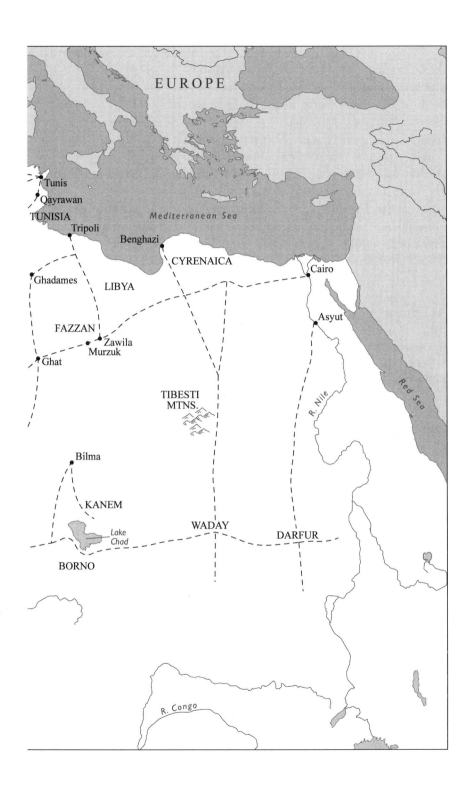

EUROPE

Mediterranean Sea

Tunis
Qayrawan
TUNISIA
Tripoli
Benghazi
CYRENAICA
Cairo
Ghadames
LIBYA
Asyut
FAZZAN
Zawila
Murzuk
Ghat
R. Nile
Red Sea
TIBESTI
MTNS.
Bilma
KANEM
WADAY
DARFUR
Lake Chad
BORNO
R. Congo

Meanwhile, the coinage systems of the Mediterranean world created a great demand for gold. A large portion of the gold from the Sudan, along with most of the production from southeast African mines, also went to India and China to purchase spices and precious textiles from societies that had little need for agricultural or manufactured imports from the Middle East or Europe. The Saharan gold trade therefore played a critical role in the medieval world economy.

The sites for producing the gold that entered Saharan trade routes lay far from the desert and at some distance from one another. The two oldest areas, Bambuk in the Senegal Valley and Buré, overlapping present-day Mali and Guinée, do not contain any major concentrations of ore. Instead, gold was extracted from shallow excavations and panned from the waters of local rivers such as the Senegal and the Niger. Even today, during the long Sudanic dry seasons when agriculture cannot be practiced, one may witness ordinary local farmers and their families trudging to local riverbanks to pan for small quantities of gold. Farther east and south, the forested lower Volta River basin holds richer deposits of ore that was extracted from deeper shafts by large groups of full-time laborers, including slaves. It is not surprising that only this area continued to be important in the modern age of industrial gold mining.

The North African merchants who crossed the Sahara never came close to the actual sources of gold and appear to have been told quite fantastic stories about its origins. Mansa Musa himself is reported to have spoken of a "gold-plant" that "blossoms after the rains...has leaves like grass and its roots are gold."[2] The trade for gold is described in several sources, including the writings of the twelfth-century Arab geographer Yaqut ibn Abd Allah, as a form of "silent" or "dumb barter" in which foreign traders "produce whatever they have brought.... Then they go away from that place a distance of one day's traveling. Then the Blacks come with the gold, put a certain amount of gold alongside each kind, and withdraw. Then the merchants come after them and each one takes the gold found beside his merchandise."[3]

Some historians think that these accounts were deliberate deceptions, designed to discourage outsiders from penetrating too far into the sub-Saharan world. Others argue that they are simply misunderstandings of information received from the Sudan by Mediterranean authors who never visited the region and imposed on it their own conceptions of an exotic and primitive world.

Arabic accounts of the gold trade are accurate in their statements about the low price paid for African gold once traders reached the Sudan. At the places of its production, gold was not even purchased with goods brought across the desert but was bartered for with commodities from within the region and, most commonly, with salt from the Sahara. Rulers such as Mansa Musa had rights to some of the gold that was brought into their domains, especially the rare nuggets (most gold was found in the form of flakes or powder that was often molded into bars). In general, however, Sudanic governments did not place heavy taxes on merchants or turn precious metals into coins. Local political authorities engaged with desert trade mainly through the capture and export of slaves.

From the beginning of the Islamic presence in the Sahara, the demand for slaves in North Africa and the Arab lands to the east preceded gold as an incentive for establishing commerce across the desert. The demand for slave labor in the Islamic world and even in parts of Mediterranean Europe continued up until 1900 and even somewhat beyond this date.

In contrast to the European colonies in the Americas, the main employment of Africans forcibly brought across the Sahara was not agriculture or other commercial activities, and the majority of the slaves were female rather than male. A substantial minority of these captives did work within the desert in the gardens and wells of oases, in salt mines, and as local caravan crews; others landed in gold mines to the south of Egypt or, during the cotton boom of the mid-1800s, on farms in Egypt itself. But the greatest number found their way into the households of wealthy and even moderately prosperous urban families, where they performed various domestic chores and also became concubines of the male household members. Another substantial minority of men, whose numbers went up and down according to political needs, served in the military forces of Muslim rulers in Egypt, North Africa, and even as far east as Iraq. Under these circumstances, enslaved people in the Islamic lands had far greater opportunities for integration into mainstream society than Africans transported to the Americas. They were often freed as a pious act when their masters died, and some, especially in military service (including eunuchs), rose to positions of great influence and power. Islamic law required that masters recognize sons born from unions with slave women and grant their mothers freedom. Some offspring of enslaved African women even became prominent rulers, including the seventeenth-century Moroccan sultan Mawlay Ismail, who based his power on a large black army. The most negative side to this relatively open-ended slavery system was the constant demand for servants to replace those who had become free (and the high percentage of black Africans who died from exposure to unfamiliar Mediterranean diets and diseases). It is also important to take into account the high death rates of the trans-Saharan forced migration, as well as the cruelty of castration operations, many of which were fatal. "Do you think anyone could forget that?" recalls an elderly former slave in twentieth-century Morocco who witnessed castrations in the caravan that brought him from southern Niger as a fourteen-year-old boy. "Even in my tomb I shall see once again the frightful spectacle of those tortured children."[4]

In contrast to the European Atlantic slave trade, scholars do not have very precise statistics for the various Islamic enslavement systems in Africa. The best estimates are that between 800 and 1900 CE about 4 million people were driven across the Sahara. Another approximately 2 million came to Egypt by way of the Nile Valley from Ethiopia and the Southern Sudan, and an additional perhaps 4 million reached the Middle East and India via the Red Sea and the Indian Ocean. This total of 10 million victims is comparable to the approximately 13 million Africans forced into ships bound for the New World; but the European slave trade occurred over a much shorter time (mainly between 1650 and 1850) and thus had a more intensive impact on Africa. The Saharan routes also brought slaves into a wide range of scattered occupations in areas (with the exception of Saharan oases) that already contained dense populations. Thus the African diaspora within the Islamic world has been less socially visible and culturally significant than its Atlantic counterpart.

Muslim legal authorities accepted sub-Saharan Africa as a legitimate source of slaves because its inhabitants were defined as *kafirun* (pagans) and therefore not under the protection of Islam. The Sudanic rulers and private raiders who captured people both for export and for local forced employment sometimes claimed to be engaged in jihad, but for the most part they appear to have been more interested in profiting from slave trading than extending or defending the frontiers of Islam. The principal asset enjoyed by most of these slavers was the horse, which allowed them to move quickly against settled populations. Horses with a worldwide reputation ("Barbary steeds") were bred in North Africa and became the most prominent import item exchanged for slaves. Other military goods, such as sword blades and armor, also came to the Sudan across the desert, but the prices of slaves on the Saharan frontiers are most often quoted in relation to horses. Ten to thirty slaves were usually required to purchase a good horse.

Slaves were exported from all regions of the Sudan throughout the history of trans-Sahara caravan trade, but more of them came from the areas east of the Niger Bend than from those farther to the west. This distinction is not due to any differences in attitude among rulers in the different regions—the Segu Empire of eighteenth- and nineteenth-century Mali was one of the most notorious slaving enterprises in all of Sudanic history—but is the result of geographical factors. In the Western Sudan until at least 1500, gold was the most valuable export, and the land between the Sahara and the Atlantic in this part of Africa is both smaller and less densely populated than areas closer to the center of the continent. The Central Sudan, by contrast, had few gold sources but access to much larger and often more heavily settled regions where more slaves could be more readily captured. There was a similar pattern in the Atlantic slave trade, which drew most of its victims from the coast between Benin and Angola, lying south of the Central Sudan, and fewer from the lands extending from present-day Ghana to Senegal, which had ties to the Western Sudan.

Gold and slaves were not the only goods sent north across the Sahara, but they were certainly the most significant for the receiving societies and probably (although this is difficult to measure) the most valuable. Another African commodity much sought after in the outside world was ivory, which could have been exported from the Sudan, a region with many elephants. However, the accounts of caravan trade before 1500 seldom mention it, in contrast to reports from the Indian Ocean, where East African ivory was always a major trade item. Medieval Arab writers do frequently make reference to large numbers of goatskins reaching the Mediterranean from the Sudan; but it is doubtful that a product of this kind, which could be found in many parts of the world, would have supported the expenses of trans-Saharan transport in this era. More likely, the establishment of trade routes for more specialized items allowed caravan traders to take on other goods such as goatskins as an added source of profit.

During the second half of the nineteenth century, goatskins and ostrich feathers became the mainstays of commerce across the desert. This was a period when little gold entered these routes and prohibitions against the slave trade began to take effect even in the Islamic world. At the same time, the hugely expanded consumer markets of industrialized Europe and America created global demands for products that had seemed trivial in earlier times. But these demands could collapse as easily as they grew. Tanned "Moroccan" (often really Sudanic) goatskins, used in clothing and bookbinding, thus enjoyed a boost in exports though other products and processes displaced them by the early decades of the twentieth century.

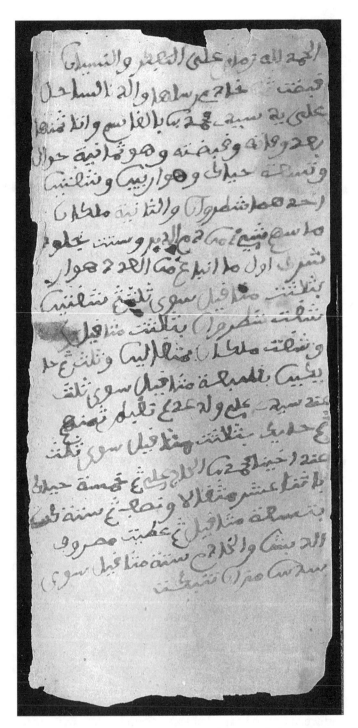

Contract setting out the terms for buying slaves from Timbuktu in Mali and transporting them to Ghadames in southern Libya. Islamic education gave trans-Saharan merchants literacy skills that they used to manage their commercial affairs. Mamma Haidara Commemorative Library

The story of ostrich feathers is more dramatic, since their export across the desert was less evident before 1850 and prices rose to dizzying heights in the 1870s, only to collapse soon afterward. The force behind this boom was a fashion in Western women's dress in the late nineteenth century that favored grand plumage of the sort uniquely provided by the ostrich, a bird native to Sudanic and Saharan Africa. In the 1880s, the profitability of the trans-Saharan feather commerce dropped sharply because of competition from domesticated ostrich farms in South Africa. North African exports of this commodity partially recovered in the 1890s, only to suffer a final blow two decades later when European and American tastes shifted to less showy dress styles. And so ended, just at the time when colonial railroads began to compete with it from another direction, the last moment of world market significance for the trans-Saharan trade.

The eclipse of caravan commerce in the era of rail, automobiles, and even early aircraft should not surprise us. More astonishing is the robust continuation over so many centuries of a transport system whose technology had hardly changed since the time of the Roman Empire. The secrets behind this endurance were two: first, the geographical barriers to trade between the Sudan and the Atlantic, and second, the efficiency with which Saharan caravan traffic was organized.

For the first six centuries of trans-Saharan trade, camel caravans enjoyed a monopoly of access to all of West and West Central Africa. The obvious alternative route to this region (and the even more isolated New World) was the South Atlantic, but none of the seafaring peoples who sailed the Mediterranean, the Indian Ocean, or the North Atlantic had yet dared to navigate these waters. Even after 1400, when the Portuguese and other Europeans began regular voyages to West Africa and established trading centers on the coast, a second barrier prevented them from competing with desert merchants for access to the savannah lands of the Sudan. The forest belt of West Africa cannot be crossed by water, because the few rivers joining it to the Sudan are blocked by rapids within seventy miles of the coast. Animal carriage through the forest was also impossible due to tropical diseases (especially sleeping sickness from the tsetse fly) that attacked not only camels but also horses, donkeys, and oxen. Until the arrival of mechanized transport, only human porters, carrying goods on their heads and backs, could be used in this region. Compared to them, camels, even though they, too, are vulnerable to the tsetse fly, proved to be an efficient commercial vehicle: as noted earlier, camels can carry more and move faster than other beasts of burden and can carry more commercial goods and fewer provisions because they can go long distances without water.

The technology of caravan transport did undergo some important developments during the first period of its introduction into the Sahara in the centuries just before and after the seventh-century Arab conquest of North Africa. Local populations learned how to raise and manage camels, and different breeds were developed: strong but somewhat slow pack camels, used in commercial caravans, and the faster and lighter saddle camels (*meharis*), employed mainly for warfare and raiding. However, once the major adaptations took place, little change seems to have occurred. A companion of Mansa Musa's 1324 pilgrimage transported to a 1900 desert crossing would have noticed no major innovation other than the addition of firearms to the caravan's weaponry. This stasis can be measured more scientifically by comparing reports of how many days it took to cross the Sahara in each period; they are effectively identical. Indeed, the caravan system seems to have consciously rejected technology that was well known in the Mediterranean world: not only the wheel but also the compass. Chariots and wagons clearly did not work very well in the Sahara. But to understand why caravan leaders did not take advantage of more sophisticated methods of navigation, it is necessary to consider the skills and resources that were necessary for carrying goods across this terrain.

The Sahara is often compared to a sea with (at least in Arabic) its "shore" (*sahel*), and the camel is likewise referred to as "the ship of the desert." Yet the best way to understand the workings of the caravan economy is to see how different it is from seafaring. To begin with, camels are not artifacts built in great cities by and for local business classes. Instead, they are animals who remain in the desert under the ownership and control of the nomadic bedouins who live there. Urban merchants did not buy camels from the bedouins but instead rented them, along with the services needed to run a caravan.

The caravans themselves, at least the major ones, were not the property of anyone but were temporary associations of several merchants. Individual and small groups of entrepreneurs created their own small caravans of camels and donkeys to bring goods from the Mediterranean to the northern Sahara trade centers. There, at specific seasons of the year, they joined together in larger groups, reloaded their property onto new animals, and crossed the main desert under the supervision of a hired leader. The camels that carried a merchant's outward-bound cargo were seldom the ones he used to bring back Sudanic goods, since the return journey involved the organization of new caravans, usually of a different size and at different times. It is this complex and fragmented nature of caravan commerce that makes it difficult to find records comparable to those of ships in the Atlantic trade.

A trans-Saharan caravan was made up of a thousand to five thousand camels and hundreds of people. Some major merchants accompanied their own goods to the Sudan, but usually men of lesser social standing undertook this arduous task. Few of those responsible for commercial matters were paid employees (thus limiting costs and the need for formal records). Instead, such work was performed by slaves, poor (often ex-slave) dependents of the merchant families, or younger relatives attempting to prove their capabilities and build up an initial stock of wealth.

Success in this arduous enterprise depended on one well-compensated professional recruited from the desert bedouins: the caravan leader. In a rare first-hand account of such a journey, an anonymous traveling merchant reports how, in about 1845, Cheggueun, one such *khebir* (guide), addressed the people of his small southern Algerian town: "I will take your sons out safely and return them in the same manner. They will make great profits. I will protect them from the Tuareg; I know the routes and the watering places, they will not suffer thirst."[5]

The caravan leader received his pay either in cash or as shares in the merchants' profits. Apart from managing the dangerous Saharan landscape (Cheggueun even provided medical services) and relationships with local populations, the leader also supervised the daily work of loading, harnessing, and feeding the camels. These tasks required a staff of paid assistants ranging from manual laborers to scouts and sometimes a Muslim clergyman to serve as the caravan chaplain.

Caravans scheduled their travel so as to avoid as much as possible the extreme heat of the Sahara. They set out only in the winter months (October to March) and even then moved only during the early part of the day or at night, using the afternoon for rest. A caravan covered, on average, fifteen to twenty-five miles per day, thus taking as long as seventy days to cross from the southern to the northern edge of the Sahara. Any specific location, such as Timbuktu, could thus expect only one or two major caravans each year.

In guiding caravans across the desert, the most important concern was to find not the shortest distance between two points but the route that provided the most security against the many threats of this dangerous terrain. Slowness or temporary loss of direction was one of these threats, since caravans carried a minimum of food in order to devote as much cargo capacity as possible to commercial items. Caravan leaders needed intimate knowledge of both the Saharan landscape and local climate, so as to predict shifts in sand dunes. They also used astronomy to take directions from stars in the clear desert sky and therefore had no need for compasses. But even the most experienced guide might get lost, since not all changes in the terrain could be foreseen, especially in the wake of sudden sandstorms. Worse, of course, was for a caravan to run directly into a sandstorm. Water remained a constant concern, and travel routes were primarily based on the distances between wells. Camels can go as long as ten days without drinking, but the usual goal was to reach water each day. There was always the possibility of arriving at a previously functional well only to find it had become dry or poisonous.

The presence of independent bedouin communities within the Sahara was at once a necessity, a threat, and an added commercial opportunity for cross-desert trade. North African merchants could not operate without trusting their goods to the camels and leadership of some group of indigenous Saharans. (Cheggueun, for example, offered an unmolested, if physically arduous, passage through his native Hoggar Mountains.) But the journey inevitably exposed merchants to the demands of other clans and chiefdoms who might attack them and have to be fought or paid off for the right of peaceful transit. Yet in many cases, trans-Saharan caravans integrated themselves into internal desert trading systems by stopping at salt production centers within the desert, such as Bilma or Tawdeni, where they could exchange some of their Mediterranean goods for salt and join with local salt transporters for the final journey to the Sudan.

The caravan system did become more efficient during the many centuries in which it flourished, in terms not of transport technology but business relations and desert politics. The major change in relations among merchants working in this part of Africa resulted from their growing involvement with Islam.

During the early period of the trans-Saharan trade, Muslim clerics in North Africa considered the Sudan to be beyond the boundaries of their own civilization and law and thus not a proper trading partner. In the course of the following centuries, Islamic influence began to spread within the Sahara and the lands to its south, and eventually Muslim merchants other than Ibadi dissidents could travel there without any stigma. Beyond making trans-Saharan trade respectable, the spread of Islam contributed to its more efficient operation. At the most basic level, Islamic education taught members of the faith to read Arabic (or at least the Arabic alphabet) thus making the keeping of written records possible. Beyond this, contractual agreements between traders or financiers drew on Islamic law, and Islamic scholars were used as judges or arbiters.

It is of course possible to carry on business without writing or formal regulations of any kind, but this limits commercial life in two ways: first, relationships are kept secure (and secret) by restricting them to people who can trust one another on the basis of personal ties, and second, if commerce is seen as very risky (as in the case of the Sahara), very high fees are charged to participants. As the influence of Islam made business more transparent and allowed trust between a wider range of business partners, costs went down. Technology also played some role here, as paper became more easily available in the Sahara due to increasingly efficient production in Europe, especially after 1800. The impact of these changes was limited, however, by what one historian has called "a paper economy of faith without faith in paper";[6] written documents were not acceptable in Islamic courts without supporting evidence from witnesses actually present before the judge.

Another of the hazards to trans-Saharan trade decreased somewhat during its later centuries as communities in the southern part of the desert became more integrated into Islamic culture and commercial life. Earlier in the history of Saharan exchange, societies from both north and south of the desert had tried to control bedouin peoples by political means. The Romans built fortifications and sent occasional expeditions into the northern Sahara. Once major points in this region, like Zawila, Wargla, and Sijilmasa had been settled by Muslims, this problem ended, even though there were sometimes conflicts between the Ibadi sects of the Sahara and authorities on the Mediterranean coast. The southern Sahara, however, remained a problem, and Sudanic states like Ghana, Songhay, and Kanem-Bornu attempted—with mixed success—to extend their power into these areas. Only after 1500, when the great days of the Sudanic empires were over, did the southern Sahara become more peaceful.

The changes came from within Saharan society rather than from outside. Like the oases of the north, the southern desert had water sources and relatively fertile highlands where small population concentrations could grow. There communities developed their own interests in conducting regular business with passing caravans as well as local trading, salt mining, and even farming where possible. The spread of Islam was also a factor here, as Mauritania, the region north of Timbuktu, and Ahir in the north of present-day Niger became important centers of both economic activity and religious study. Besides assuring more support and security for traders crossing the desert, these stabilized Saharan communities also provided important markets for the growing commercial economies of the Sudan.

"I have been informed," wrote the ninth-century geographer Ahmad ibn Abi Yaqub al-Yaqubi, "that the kings of the Sudan sell their people without any pretext of war."[7] Thus for Mediterranean observers already somewhat prejudiced against black Africans, the fact that they did not seem to know the value of gold and readily exported slaves implied a very low level of economic development. Within the boundaries of the Sahara and Sudan, however, long-distance trade, even in slaves, stimulated a rich and varied local economy involving the exchange of many agricultural and mineral goods, large-scale urban handicraft industries, and wide-ranging merchant networks.

Well before the first camel caravans crossed the desert, Saharan and Sudanic peoples had been trading salt, dates, and copper from the north for fish and cereal grains from the south. Global trade increased the range and quantity of this regional commerce. Sudanic merchants brought desert salt far into the interior of West Africa in payment for gold. Other local farm products that could travel well, including onions, cotton, leather and hides, kola nuts (a local source of caffeine), and, after it was introduced to the region from the New World, tobacco, also entered these trade circuits. Many (perhaps most) of the people captured in slave raids also were kept within the region, sometimes serving as local military forces but more often performing agricultural work around the major Sudanic cities and in the centers of Saharan settlement. In both the desert and regions to the south, Islamic scholars supported themselves by employing students and slaves as laborers on commercial farms.

Although the Sudan imported manufactures from the Mediterranean in return for raw materials, local cities such as Timbuktu and Kano eventually began to produce their own goods to compete with or complement commodities that came in from the north. Cotton textiles were the most important of these commodities. They had a wide local and export market, they were made from a plant that grew abundantly in the Sudan itself, and the skills of spinning thread and weaving cloth could be quickly learned. The major limit on Sudanic cottons was their color; they had to be either white or blue, as the only dye available on a large scale in the region came from the indigo plant. However, these cottons met most local needs and could successfully compete with imports not only in West Africa but also in much of the Sahara, where Tuareg populations came to be identified by their dark blue garments.

The role of leather in the Sudanic economy is more complicated. This commodity was simultaneously exported raw, turned into commercial manufactured goods, and used to add value to imported goods.

Trans-Saharan caravans regularly carried cattle hides and especially goatskins to North Africa. At the same time, Sudanic artisans produced tanned leather and even leather goods such as sandals and cushions for both local consumption and export. Finally, the same craftsmen manufactured leather sheaths for the imported blades of swords (with wooden handles produced by local blacksmiths).

The impact of desert trade extended even beyond the Sudan into Nigerian forest areas near the Atlantic coast such as Ife, Igbo Ukwu, and ancient Benin in Nigeria. We know little about how copper from the Sahara first arrived in these distant regions. Archaeological evidence indicates that from as early as the tenth century CE, local artisans mixed it with tin and zinc (obtained nearby) to make bronze and brass artworks of great beauty and often monumental size.

North African merchants seldom, if ever, traveled beyond the cities immediately south of the desert. Real or imagined dangers might explain initial hesitations to enter this unfamiliar environment; but over the long run the disincentives probably arose from recognition that such ventures required a very different set of transport technologies and cultural skills than desert travel. The task of connecting the end points of the caravans with savannah and forest zone sources of export goods thus became the specialty of indigenous Sudanic traders.

The history of Sudanic merchants shows how professional, ethnic, and religious identities can merge and change to adapt themselves to new conditions. Communities of these entrepreneurs developed close to the commercial centers of the Sahel (the semidesert fringe of the Sahara that stretches from Mauritania to Chad) because of their relationship with Saharan caravans. However, over the long development of trans-Saharan trade, the major contact points for North African merchants expanded from west to east. During the early centuries of this commerce, caravans seeking gold headed to Ghana and Takrur, located west of the Niger River and closest to the earliest source of precious metal exports, Bambuk. The populations in this region spoke the Soninke language, and they established interior trade routes along a southwestern axis.

To this day peoples of Soninke origin remain dispersed all over West Africa, but more as peasant farmers and migrant laborers (even extending into Europe) than as merchants. The Soninke explain their fallen status, as well as the collapse of their former empire of Ghana, by telling the story of a monstrous snake, Bida, who promised them prosperity and power so long they offered him a virgin girl each year. When the suitor of one of these girls intervened and killed Bida, the dying snake pronounced a curse that caused the land to dry up and its people to be scattered.

Historians treat the myth of Bida as the memory of a drought that struck the Soninke homelands somewhere between the twelfth and fourteenth centuries. During that time, caravans began to move more toward the east and south, seeking cities on or close to the Niger River such as Timbuktu, Dia, and Gao. From there, Sudanic merchant networks began to move directly south into the newer gold fields of Buré in southern Mali and northern Guinée. The languages here are variants of Mande (Bambara and Malinke), and these became the ethnic markers of merchant communities, even those who were descendants of Soninke-speakers. The names used for these trading groups indicate their complicated origin. They are most commonly called Juula (sometimes spelled Dyula or Dioula), a Mande word meaning merchants. But in some parts of West Africa they were also known as Wangara, a term used in the early Arabic accounts to refer to Soninke-speaking people and the lands south of Ghana.

From the fifteenth century onward, the Juula shifted their activities further to the east. Their main source of gold now became the Volta River basin in the forest zone of modern Ghana. Within the Sudanic savannah, merchants in the Songhay capital of Gao also opened up routes into the cities and densely populated farmlands of the Hausa people in present-day Niger and northern Nigeria. The initial attraction of this region had nothing directly to do with trans-Saharan trade, since Hausaland did not establish an independent connection with the Mediterranean before 1400. Instead, the Hausa provided the Western Sudan with a valuable market for both imported and locally manufactured goods. In return, they exported slaves and salt products. Eventually, a second Juula route to Hausaland was opened from the Volta basin. This trade involved some gold but mainly focused on kola nuts, a caffeine stimulant in great demand throughout the Sudan for both local consumption and export northward. Kola nuts were grown only in the forest regions to the south.

By the 1700s, Hausa-speaking merchants took over much of this commerce and spread their own trading diasporas over the Central Sudan and the neighboring forest zones of present-day Ghana, Nigeria, and Cameroon. As with the population shift from Soninke to Juula, some of these traders were the offspring of Mande who had simply taken on a new language. In the Hausa case, we can more easily follow the changes of ethnicity, as merchant lineages here maintain oral traditions of their origins. One such group is even called Wangara, while others trace their ancestry to communities closer to Hausaland, including Berber-speakers of the south-central Sahara and immigrants from Borno to the east.

The one identity shared by all merchants in this broad commercial system stretching from the Mediterranean throughout West Africa is Islam. However, in the Sudan, being Muslim was at once more closely associated with the profession of trading than in North Africa and at the same time did not so closely govern the management of commercial relationships. The early Juula and Hausa merchants converted to Islam but did not have access to the kind of learning that would have allowed them to submit their business dealings to the detailed regulations of economic life laid down by the Shariah, the legal code of their new religion. Sudanic societies did eventually produce their own centers of Islamic scholarship, but even these did not train their students to become arbiters of economic affairs. Within the Sudanic merchant communities, very little use was made of written records, and the regulation of credit or partnerships depended almost entirely on personal relations rather than formal rules.

Up until the 1400s, Muslims had been the only outsiders to enter the African lands south of the Sahara. Beginning with the Portuguese voyages of Atlantic discovery, however, European Christians also became a presence in this landscape. In physical and cultural terms, Europeans remained marginal to the Sahara and neighboring Sudan well up into the 1800s. With the exception a few individual explorers, they stayed on the coast and often carried on trade without even leaving their ships. Very few West Africans converted to Christianity during this period. Nevertheless, the opening of a new Atlantic commercial frontier did have an immediate and profound impact on the economic life of the West African interior.

The export goods sought by Europeans were essentially the same as those that flowed across the Sahara, primarily gold and slaves, but they also sought such other goods as ivory, tropical hardwood, and gum arabic. In the case of gold, West African forest producers benefited from the availability of Atlantic routes while Saharan commerce diminished. The Atlantic slave trade, on the other hand, caused horrendous suffering to its West African victims, but nonetheless stimulated greater commercial activity in the Sudan and Sahara, bringing material gains to all those who profited from the trade.

By the time Europeans arrived on the Atlantic African coast, the principal source of trans-Saharan gold exports had shifted southeastward from Senegal and Mali to the Volta River basin. It did not take the Portuguese long to discover this fact, and in 1482 they built their first permanent structure on the neighboring coast, a massive fortress named

São Jorge da Mina (St. George of the Mine, now called Elmina Castle). When local trade was taken over by the northern Europeans and even after this region became a British colony, it was called the Gold Coast (now Ghana).

The Europeans enjoyed great advantages over their North African rivals both in having trading locations closer to the gold mines than were the Sahelian caravan destinations and in the greater efficiency of ships compared to camels. The flow of precious metal did not, however, shift immediately or completely to the coast. In the beginning, contact with the gold producers remained in the hands of Juula merchants, and the Portuguese took some time to provide import goods that could compete effectively with Sudanic cloth. But eventually something like three-quarters of the gold produced in West Africa left by the Atlantic route.

Within the Sahara, a new gold trade route from the Central Sudan actually developed after 1500. This was the result of contact between Hausa merchants and the Volta region, which brought gold directly to such cities as Kano and Birni Ngazargamo in Borno, whence North African merchants carried it across the desert to Libya and Egypt. In the Western Sudan, Timbuktu and Jenne received much less gold than previously from the Volta mines but could still tap into the continual but less intensive production in the Senegal and Niger basins. North African imports of gold thus fell off considerably during the early 1500s. In order to reverse this decline, the Moroccan sultan Ahmad al-Mansur al-Dhahabi ("the Golden") sent armies into the Sahara and the Sudan to take over salt mines and, finally, to conquer the Songhay Empire. The resulting revival of the Moroccan gold trade was short-lived, and over the next two centuries, the flow of precious metal in this direction fell back to more modest levels. By the 1800s, trans-Saharan gold cargoes everywhere were much reduced and irregular, often consisting of no more than a few feather quills of dust, carried as supplements to other commodities.

For the first century or more of European trade with West Africa, gold was the main object of commerce and slaves only secondary. At Elmina, the Portuguese even imported slaves from the Congo region in order to exchange them for gold. From about 1650 to 1850, however, slaves dominated West African Atlantic exports, reaching a level with no parallel in human history. Two of the regions that supplied the greatest number of these captives—the Congo River basin and the Bight of Biafra—had not been part of the Sahara-Sudan commercial network. However, a significant number of slaves also came from zones that were closely linked to Muslim trading routes, including Senegambia, the Bight of Benin, and—in a direct reversal of earlier European trends—the Gold Coast (which

A merchant (flanked by a nobleman and an interpreter) from the Volta River valley of central Ghana appears on the Atlantic Gold Coast in the late 1500s. In this period, the Volta region was the main source for trans-Saharan gold exports, which suffered a major blow from competition with European shippers. Source: Pieter de Morees, Beschryvinshe ende historiche verhael van Gout Koninchkrijk van Gunea *(Gravenhage: M. Nijhoff, 1912 [original 1602]).* Courtesy Joseph Regenstein Library, University of Chicago

now imported some New World gold in exchange for slaves). Nonetheless, there is no evidence that the slave trade across the Sahara decreased during this period and even reason to believe it grew.

There are several explanations for the lack of competition between the Saharan and the Atlantic slave trades. Most obvious are the complementary gender demands of the two labor markets. The Islamic world sought mainly domestic servants and thus favored females over males. European plantations in the New World, on the other hand, very explicitly required that two-thirds of all Africans brought to them be males. Contact with the Americas also had one positive social impact that, at least partially, compensated for the huge drain of African population. This was the introduction of new food crops, particularly cassava (also called manioc), maize (American corn), and peanuts. With such added sources of nutrition, African lands could support a greater number of people and thus lessen the demographic impact of forced emigration across two frontiers at the same time.

The social costs of the Atlantic slave trade were mainly felt in the forest zones of West and Central Africa, where most of the victims were captured. However, slave raids also took place in the Sudan, and about 10 percent of the Africans who survived being shipped to the New World were Muslims. Moreover, the two centuries of intensive slave trade brought a general increase in violence that spread across all of West Africa. Along with the horses, sword blades, and armor that came across the Sahara in exchange for slaves, the Atlantic trade now supplied guns, which added to the militarization of the entire region. The religious wars that broke out among Muslims in the Sudan—beginning in the late 1600s—were partially incited by increased slave trading and also provided more captives, augmenting both the Atlantic and Saharan slave markets.

Along with all the human misery and disorder that resulted from the forcible removal of large numbers of people from their homelands, the Atlantic trade brought some economic advantages to West Africa. Competition between purchasers arriving via the sea and the desert, as well as among the different European buyers, continually raised the price of slaves, materially benefiting the African sellers and their societies. Some import goods, such as cloth and iron, competed with local products, but consumer tastes and markets also expanded, thus contributing to a growth in, among other things, the Sudanic textile industry and its exports into the Sahara. On the Mediterranean side of the desert, European economic activity also grew during this period, enlarging markets for such caravan goods as ivory, goatskins, ostrich feathers, and even gold.

One European import that clearly helped West African economic development was cowrie shells. These small objects, harvested at very low cost from mollusks in the Maldive Islands southwest of India, had been brought to the Sudan in limited quantities by trans-Saharan caravans prior to 1500 and continued to be imported across the desert in later centuries. However, Dutch and British ships trading with India could carry larger quantities of cowries more cheaply than desert traders, and in fact they needed heavy items of this kind in their holds to assure stability on the long voyages back to Europe. For Africans, the shells sometimes served decorative and ritual purposes, as in the crowns of sacred kings in present-day Nigeria (not coincidently the same forest region that imported Saharan copper for artistic use). But the most important economic function of cowries in West Africa was their wide circulation as monetary currency.

Other forms of money existed in the region at this time, including imported coins and various commodities with other uses, such as cloth strips or iron bars. Cowries had the unique advantage, however, of being relatively cheap, small, durable, and difficult to counterfeit. They have been employed in many parts of the world for small transactions in place of impractical bartering. Such exchanges became necessary when people traveled away from home to marketplaces where they needed to deal with strangers for minor services such as food, temporary shelter, entertainment, or the carrying of goods. In West Africa, cowrie currencies circulated in a broad zone extending eastward from the Gold Coast to the Niger Delta and north into most of the West and Central Sudan, as well as to some points in the southern Sahara.

With the addition of Atlantic imports to those from across the Sahara, the price of cowries in the Sudan fell by half, from three thousand to a *mithqal* (the standard measure of gold) down to fifteen hundred. However, the fact that this new ratio remained stable for about three hundred years, despite an ever-increasing money supply, indicates that West African and linked Saharan economies must have been growing throughout the era of the slave trade.

By the mid-1800s, the cowrie currency did go into crisis because of a radical jump in the European import of the shells, which now came from not only India but also new sources in East Africa. In its place, alternative forms of money entered West Africa by both caravan and ship, especially European silver and copper coins such as the Austrian Maria Theresa thaler (or dollar), the British shilling and penny, and the French 5-franc piece. Such wealth continued to flow in because the end of the slave trade coincided with European demand for new "legitimate" (i.e., nonhuman) commodities of various kinds from Africa.

One such item, gum arabic, duplicated to some extent the role of gold by diverting trade from the Sahara. This resin came from acacia trees in Mauritania, north of the Senegal River where the Sahara meets the Atlantic Ocean. According to a local oral tradition, Europeans first learned about the value of gum arabic in Gibraltar, where they met a young Mauritanian who had crossed the desert to pursue Muslim learning and said he remained healthy by following his mother's advice "to eat three pieces before each meal."[8] This account captures the early, limited appeal of gum arabic in both the Islamic and Western worlds as food, medicine, cosmetic, and a component of manufacturing. Demand among Europeans exploded in the 1700s, when they began manufacturing cotton textiles in competition with India and needed gum arabic to produce the needed vibrant colors. The subsequent rise in gum exports provided major income for peoples living on the edge of the Sahara, but it was exported overseas almost entirely by Atlantic ship rather than by desert caravan.

Ivory, another minor item in earlier trans-Saharan trade, became more prominent in caravan cargoes during the 1700s and especially the 1800s. The major reason for this change was the growing European demand for items made of elephant tusk, including not only traditional decorative articles but also piano keys and billiard balls. It might seem more cost-efficient for most of this ivory to reach Europe directly by way of the Atlantic, and much of it certainly did (one West African country still bears the name Ivory Coast). In the regions from Cameroon to the south, however, Muslim Hausa traders gave strong competition to European merchants, and during some years of the nineteenth century as much ivory crossed the desert as the ocean.

The other West African commodities purchased by European shippers, mainly peanuts, the oil and seeds of the palmetto palm, and wild rubber, had too little value in relation to bulk to make them worth carrying long distances to the desert or across it by camel. Even in these cases, however, the exports of the forest zones contributed to the economic growth of the Western and Central Sudan. Prosperous coastal societies provided expanded markets for Sudanic agricultural and manufactured goods and brought valuable imports, such as cowrie currency, into the regions at the edge of the desert. Moreover, the production of Atlantic export goods created new demands for Sudanic labor, in the form of either slaves who were used to cultivate, transport, and protect routes for palm products or seasonal voluntary migrants who labored in the peanut zones of Senegal.

The strengthened Sudanic markets in turn sustained the continuation of trade into and across the Sahara. Given the cost of transport through the forest zone from the Atlantic, even European cotton goods could still be imported economically by Mediterranean-based camel caravans. Some African goods also reached Europe and the Middle East by the same routes. What finally reduced trans-Saharan trade to a very small scale was the introduction of European colonial rule and mechanized transportation systems that linked the coast and the Sudan. Even then, camel caravans continued to carry some important desert commodities, such as the salt so needed by savannah farmers and herders.

As a major factor in the world economy, the trans-Saharan routes were eclipsed soon after 1500. But the character of global developments is not as uniform as we often think. In the case of the precolonial Sahara and Sudan, new oceanic linkages actually stimulated the growth of regional exchange economies at the same time that they made them less important to the outside world. These economies in turn continued to sustain important developments in politics, religion, and general culture.

CHAPTER 3

Ruling the Sahara and Its "Shores"

ew events in the distant past of trans-Saharan Africa can be tied to exact dates, because most business in this region transpired without the use of written records. There is one major exception: a battle at a place called Tondibi on the Niger River, where an invading Moroccan expedition encountered the forces of the Songhay Empire. "They fought there on Tuesday, March 13, 1591," a chronicler from Timbuktu tells us, "and the troops of [the Moroccan commander] Juwadar broke the army of the Askiya [Songhay ruler] in the twinkling of an eye."[1]

This confrontation did not just catch the attention of contemporary Mediterranean and Sudanic authors; many modern historians see it as a turning point in trans-Saharan history. In economic terms, the battle was linked to the diversion of gold trade from the desert to Atlantic Ocean routes. It marks the end of the great medieval states of the Western Sudan (Songhay being the successor to legendary Ghana and Mali) and the beginning of the early modern era, signaled by the firearms that produced the Moroccan victory. It is also a rare, if not unique, moment of truly trans-Saharan political struggle.

Like the stories told by Mansa Musa nearly 270 years earlier in Cairo, the drama of Tondibi is both revealing and deceptive. It tells us that politics played a major role in efforts to control trade routes and access to precious commodities but does not indicate how such control could be effectively exercised. It underlines the importance of a new European presence on the west coast of Africa, but distorts both the economic and political consequences of this change. It shows that Maghrib states remained more technologically advanced than their Sudanic counterparts but exaggerates the degree of this difference and its significance. In short, no serious scholar thinks that history can be explained by "kings and battles," yet political events are important in themselves and, because of their visibility, provide useful indicators of broader issues.

During the eleven centuries of flourishing trans-Saharan trade, a great number of empires, states, and dynasties rose and fell in both the

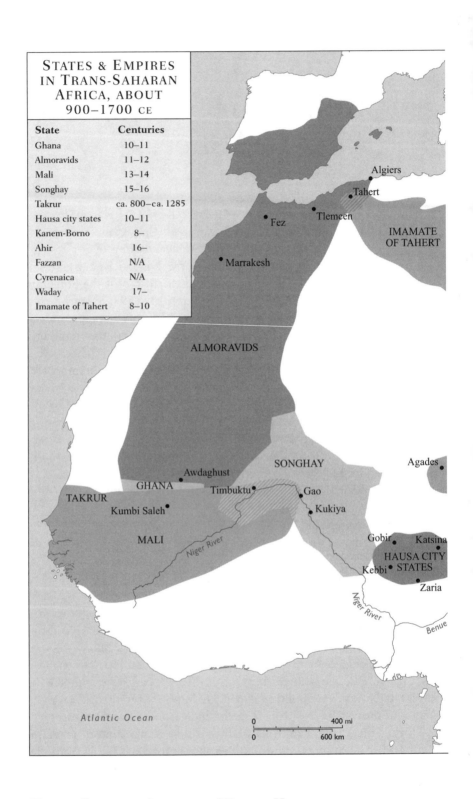

STATES & EMPIRES
IN TRANS-SAHARAN
AFRICA, ABOUT
900–1700 CE

State	Centuries
Ghana	10–11
Almoravids	11–12
Mali	13–14
Songhay	15–16
Takrur	ca. 800–ca. 1285
Hausa city states	10–11
Kanem-Borno	8–
Ahir	16–
Fazzan	N/A
Cyrenaica	N/A
Waday	17–
Imamate of Tahert	8–10

Algiers

Tahert

Tlemcen

Fez

IMAMATE
OF TAHERT

Marrakesh

ALMORAVIDS

Agades

SONGHAY

Awdaghust

GHANA

Timbuktu

Gao

TAKRUR

Kumbi Saleh

Kukiya

MALI

Niger River

Gobir

Katsina

HAUSA CITY
STATES

Kebbi

Zaria

Niger River

Benue

Atlantic Ocean

0				400 mi

0				600 km

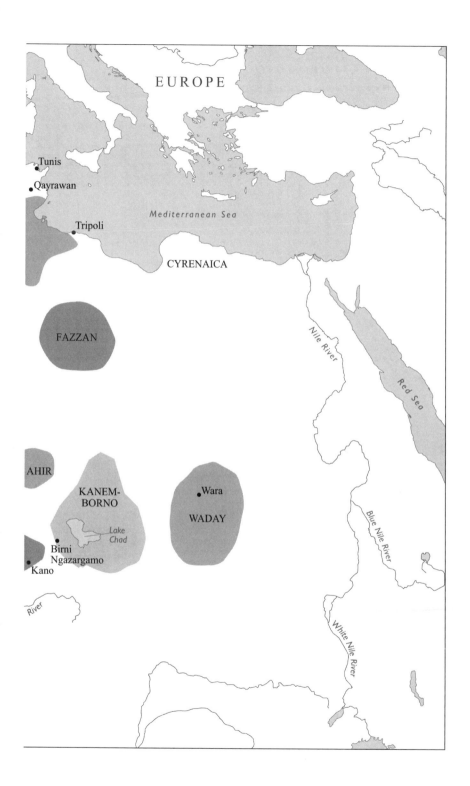

EUROPE

Tunis

Qayrawan

Tripoli

Mediterranean Sea

CYRENAICA

Nile River

Red Sea

FAZZAN

AHIR

KANEM-
BORNO

Wara

WADAY

*Lake
Chad*

Birni
Ngazargamo

Kano

River

Blue Nile River

White Nile River

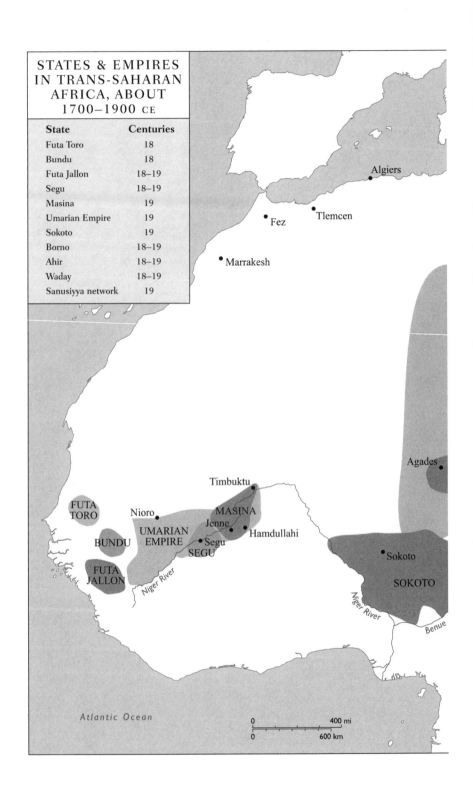

STATES & EMPIRES
IN TRANS-SAHARAN
AFRICA, ABOUT
1700–1900 CE

State	Centuries
Futa Toro	18
Bundu	18
Futa Jallon	18–19
Segu	18–19
Masina	19
Umarian Empire	19
Sokoto	19
Borno	18–19
Ahir	18–19
Waday	18–19
Sanusiyya network	19

Algiers

Tlemcen

Fez

Marrakesh

Agades

Timbuktu

FUTA
TORO

Nioro

MASINA

Jenne

Hamdullahi

UMARIAN
EMPIRE

BUNDU

Segu

SEGU

Sokoto

FUTA
JALLON

SOKOTO

Niger River

Niger River

Benue

Atlantic Ocean

0   400 mi
0   600 km

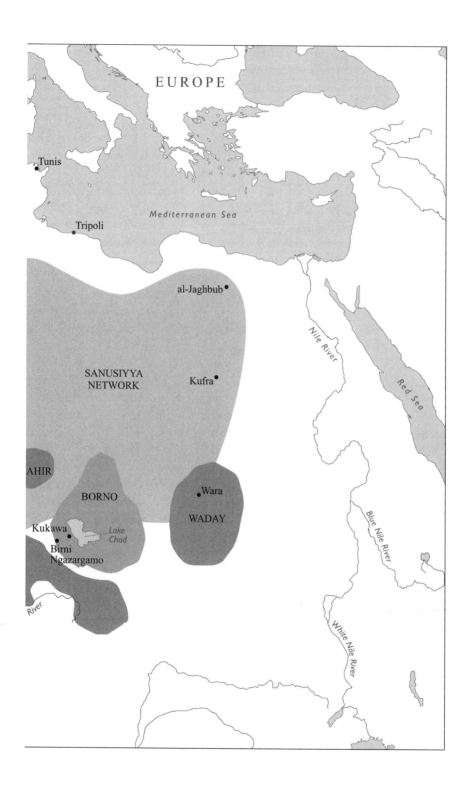

EUROPE

Tunis

Tripoli

Mediterranean Sea

al-Jaghbub

Nile River

Red Sea

SANUSIYYA
NETWORK

Kufra

AHIR

BORNO

Wara

WADAY

Kukawa

*Lake
Chad*

Birni
Ngazargamo

Blue Nile River

River

White Nile River

Maghrib and the Western and Central Sudan. Desert commerce did not always play a central role in these politics, especially for the Maghrib, with its direct access to the rich economies of the Mediterranean and Egypt. But caravan traffic was an essential condition for the emergence of powerful political centers in the Sudan. Moreover, not only did rulers to the north and south fight to control the Sahara but the desert also produced its own political dynamics, sometimes with major repercussions for the more densely populated regions on its borders.

For most of the Islamic era, the Maghrib was divided into small, often warring, states roughly corresponding to the present-day divisions between Morocco, Algeria, Tunisia, and Libya. Only in Morocco and Libya did Mediterranean coastal rulers make efforts to control neighboring portions of the Sahara. Even the rural areas between the coast and the desert proved difficult to manage, especially after the eleventh century, when two Arab bedouin tribes, the Hilali and Sulaim, invaded the Maghrib from Egypt.

The most lasting effect these nomads had on rural North Africa was their imposition of the Arabic language and a new ethnic identity on the majority of local Berber populations. By the fourteenth century, branches of this invading force also migrated into the Western Sahara, where they came to dominate the local Sanhaja Berber communities and assimilate them into a common Arab-speaking community as "Moors," or Bidan (whites). Beginning in the twelfth century, other Arab nomads entered the southeastern Sahara from the Nilotic Sudan and migrated westward to Lake Chad. However, the large central portions of the desert and its southern borders between Timbuktu and Kawar remained under the control of Berber-speaking Tuareg tribesmen, who founded their own Saharan state of Agades in the Ahir Plateau in the 1500s.

The political history of the Western and Central Sudan is more difficult to write than that of North Africa because of the paucity of documentation. None of the governments there kept records of their day-to-day operations, though greater commitment to Islam did increase the general use of writing, as in the realm of commerce. From the later period of the Songhay Empire onward (starting in 1500) residents of these states, usually Islamic clergy but occasionally the rulers themselves, produced some correspondence and chronicles. For the most part, however, historians must rely on the writings of foreign travelers. In the early period of exclusively North African contact with the Sudan, a few Muslim scholars actually visited the region, while some stay-at-home geographers gathered information from trans-Saharan merchants, clergy, and Sudanese pilgrims. Beginning in the late 1400s, European explorers also produced reports on the region.

The other major accounts of Sudanic rulers come from oral traditions, usually recorded long after the events they describe and subject to many motivations other than helping scholars find out what actually happened in the past. However, they often do preserve revealing images of important rulers. Finally, as for the pre-Islamic period, significant information can be gathered from archeological research, although in some cases, for example Mali, no one has figured out exactly where to look for the cities described in written and oral texts.

Of all the great Sudanic states, Ghana is the one about which historians have the least knowledge. Its capital, established by Soninke-speaking peoples in the tenth century, was definitely located west of the Niger Bend and served as a center for gold trade from both Bambuk and Buré. The name Ghana, derived from Arabic writings, has been taken by a modern African state (the former Gold Coast) located far from the Sahara. But in the Soninke oral traditions of the snake Bida and its curse of drought, the empire that collapsed is remembered as Wagadu and its rulers are called Cisse. Neither of these terms appears in any medieval North African sources.

Closer to Bambuk there was at least one other important state, Takrur, which had independent relations with trans-Saharan traders. For much of the medieval era, "Takrur" was even used by Arab sources as the name for the entire Western Sudan. Nonetheless, the twelfth-century geographer Abu Abd Allah al-Idrisi describes Ghana as "the greatest of all the towns of the Sudan" and gives detailed, if probably exaggerated, accounts of the wealth and power of its kings.[2]

Climatic change does explain the long-term eclipse of Ghana; the ruins of its probable capital, Kumbi Saleh, lie at an abandoned site on the expanded southwestern edge of the Sahara. A more immediate factor may have been an early trans-Saharan confrontation: a competition for control of strategic points farther north in the desert with the Berber empire of the Almoravids. By the beginning of the eleventh century, Ghana had established some kind of hegemony over Awdaghust, the oasis in the southern Sahara then serving as a well-populated center of agriculture and caravan trade in gold and salt. The Almoravid regime, which ruled Morocco and southern Spain in the early twelfth century, had its origins in the 1050s among the Sanhaja Berbers of this desert region. Once organized around the charismatic religious leader Abd Allah ibn Yasin, the Sanhaja took over first the northern desert portal of Sijilmasa and then Awdaghust in the south. Eventually the Almoravids directed their main energies toward the Mediterranean. But a southern branch of the movement continued to dominate the western Sahara and by the end of the eleventh century attacked Ghana itself.

Historians remain in dispute over whether the Almoravids actually conquered Ghana and converted its rulers to Islam. Ghana did, in any case, survive in some form through the 1100s. The drying out of western Mauritania, which included both Ghana and Awdaghust, took place only in the thirteenth century. During the immediately preceding era, Ghana suffered not just assaults from Saharan Berbers but also rivalry with neighboring Sudanic states and probably conquest by a rival Soninke people, the Susu. For all these reasons, the center of power in the Western Sudan now shifted to locations closer to the Niger River and gold sources lying farther east.

The first new empire was Mali, also revived as the name of a postcolonial state but one much closer to the location of its medieval predecessor. Mali, centered in the forest-savannah of the southern Niger basin, is the farthest from the Sahara of all the medieval Western Sudanic states. Its Malinke people, unlike the Soninke of old Ghana, were never forced to move due to ecological catastrophe.

There is also a good deal of written information about Mali, from the recorded statements of Mansa Musa and other medieval pilgrims to North Africa and the first-hand travel account of Shams ad-Din Ibn Battuta, who praises "the security embracing the whole country, so that neither traveler there nor dweller has anything to fear from either thief or usurper."[3] The rich Malinke oral traditions tell us about a long line of rulers extending well past the time of Mali's greatness into the lineages of smaller successor chiefdoms that still exist today under the dynastic name Keita. For the thirteenth and fourteenth centuries, such accounts give less emphasis to Mansa Musa than to the founder of the empire, Sunjata. But what Malinke griots (bards) have to say about Sunjata— "Master Hunter, Lion-Born-of-the-Cat"—belongs more to the realm of literature and anthropology than political history.

At its height, in the fourteenth-century era of Mansa Musa, Mali's sovereignty covered a vast portion of the Sudan—"its length being four months journey and its width likewise," according to a long-term Arab resident cited by the Egyptian scholar Ibn Fadl Allah al-Umari.[4] This territory included the Atlantic coasts of Senegal and the Gambia as well as Sahelian zone of the Niger Bend and even extended as far as the trading centers of Walata in the western desert and Tadmekka in the south central Sahara. Mali did not, however, exercise direct control over its gold sources, either Buré (very close to the center of the empire) or the more distant Volta River basin. The same informant of al-Umari reported that "as soon as one of them [the Mali kings] conquers one of the gold towns and Islam spreads...the gold there begins to decrease."[5]

The best explanation for the decline of Mali and its eclipse by Song-hay in the late fourteenth century is overexpansion. Mali, at its height, claimed more territory than any other Western Sudanic empire, and it was inevitable that distant provinces would eventually break away when the strong rulers who had conquered them were succeeded by less able individuals, or when rivalries for power divided the dynasty.

With the rise of the Songhay Empire, political power in the Western Sudan shifted back to the desert edge, but in this case to a relatively fertile location on the middle reaches of the Niger River. The history of Songhay is much better documented by archaeology and written sources than that of its predecessors, Ghana and Mali.

Gao, the eventual political capital of Songhay, had been an important center of Saharan trade even before the Islamic era and became an early attraction for trans-Saharan commerce. By the ninth century its first rulers, the Za dynasty, took control over the territory around the city. The prosperity of this state and its Sonrai population attracted the attention of the Mali Empire, which conquered the region around the end of the thirteenth century and ruled there until the early fifteenth century. The dynasty that displaced Mali as the dominant power over the Middle Niger bore the name of Sunni and had earlier been based at Kukiya, a trading center to the southeast of Gao. Its last ruler, Sunni Ali Ber ("the Great") is remembered in the Muslim chronicles of Tim-buktu (which became a second Songhay capital) as both an effective conqueror and administrator and a very evil man, "a tyrant, a miscre-ant, an aggressor, a despot, and a butcher who killed so many human beings that only God Most High could count them."[6] Whether this description is accurate or a form of propaganda for the next Songhay regime remains unclear.

The same chroniclers tell us that shortly after Sunni Ali died in 1492, one of his governors "nursed an ambition to gain power," and "after he had finished tying together the strands of his various schemes," took over the empire under the name Askia Muhammad. Linguistic evidence suggests that this new ruler was most likely of slave origin, but the chronicles, written by the successors to scholars befriended by Askia Muhammad, call him "the most felicitous and well-guided one."[7] Whatever the social status or virtue of its founder, the emergent Askia dynasty presided over the most glorious period in Songhay's history.

During the 1500s, this empire extended north into the Sahara as far as the Taghaza oasis, west almost to the Senegal River, and east into the Hausa town of Kebbi, but south only to the edge of the core Malinke ethnic region, where a small Mali state still survived. While internal divisions and resistance at the Sudanic frontiers periodically weakened Songhay during this time, the collapse of the state came from its rivalry with Morocco over Saharan gold and salt trade.

Ahmad al-Mansur, the Moroccan sultan who invaded the Middle Niger in 1591, claimed to be acting in the interests of not only his own country but the entire Islamic world. As he told a somewhat skeptical state council before launching his trans-Saharan expedition, "The Sudan, being a very rich country and providing enormous revenues, we can now increase the size of the armies of Islam and strengthen the battalions of the faithful."[8] In the event, al-Mansur's troops routed the Songhay forces at the battle of Tondibi, and the sultan did at first receive large quantities of gold, mainly the result of looting by the North African forces. Within a few years, this source of wealth proved as disappointing as had been al-Mansur's earlier occupation of salt mines within the desert itself. By 1618, a new Moroccan sultan decided to leave his representatives in the distant south to their own devices.

The resulting Sudanic regime is known as Arma (from Arabic *ar-rumah*, meaning musketeers or shooters) because of its signature weaponry. But the military power of these conquerors did not produce a stable or strong government. Instead, various families contended for power, often quite violently, so that between 1691 and the end of the regime in 1833 no fewer than 167 pashas succeeded one another. At their best moments, up to the mid-1600s, the Arma controlled the key commercial centers of Timbuktu (their capital) and Jenne. However, they were continuously assaulted from the Sahara by Tuareg Berber nomads and eventually from the savannah by new Sudanic empires: first the Bambara of Segu and then the Fulani of Masina.

The Bambara are a northward extension of the Mande-speaking Malinke people who had earlier founded the Mali Empire. Their own empire was rooted in a reaction against trans-Saharan trade, specifically its demands for slaves. The Bambara built their state upon a village institution, the *ton*, a fellowship of young men who have been circumcised at the same time but are not yet married. Under normal circumstances, the main function of a *ton* is to help with the heavy work of grain harvesting. In situations of danger, it can also become a village military organization. In the 1600s, with slave trade from both the Sahara and the Atlantic rising, the military aspects of the *ton* became dominant. Segu and its neighboring villages consolidated their forces around the leadership of a single family, the Coulibaly, and a new political regime was born.

Segu only began to become a serious power in the 1710s under the rule of the legendary Biton Coulibaly, remembered in Bambara epics not for defending his people from the slave trade but as "the Hunter of Men." Biton's innovation was not only to capture and sell slaves (*jon* in the Mande language) but also to incorporate some of them into the *ton* as a permanent army, the *tonjon*. Following Biton's death in 1755, a leading member of the *tonjon*, Ngolo Jara, took over the state, founding a new dynasty that endured until the collapse of Segu in 1861.

Segu oral traditions focus on the high point of the empire under Ngolo's grandson, Da Monzon, who ruled from 1808 to 1827. Da Monzon directly controlled the Middle Niger region from Bamako to Masina and exercised influence over a wide region of the Western Sudan. As indicated by Da Monzon's praise name, "Master of the Waters, Master of Men, Master of Powder, and Master of Iron," the regime drew its strength from a combination of traditional powers (particularly the water spirits associated with Biton Coulibaly) and the more modern resource of "(gun)powder." What eventually brought Segu down was a new force from across the Sahara, political Islam.

The movements that created religious-based states in the Western and Central Sudan from the 1600s through the 1800s are commonly referred to as jihads (Arabic for "struggle" but understood in West Africa as holy wars). In the rest of the Muslim world, the term was not often used in this sense until the late twentieth century, but its principle, the mobilization of warriors behind preachers of Islam, is best exemplified by the career of the Prophet Muhammad himself and lay behind the original penetration of North Africa and the Sahara by Arab armies. Muslim clerics were also the founders of the Almoravid Empire, as well as the Moroccan dynasty of Ahmad al-Mansur, the sixteenth-century conqueror of Songhay.

Within the Sudan, politics driven by jihad developed later and initially on a more limited basis, although Islamic holy men eventually founded quite powerful empires in this region as well. All these movements had three elements in common: reformist religious doctrines, increasingly tied to Sufi mystical brotherhoods; ethnic conflicts, usually between pastoralists speaking the Fulani language and local agricultural populations; and conditions of increasing economic prosperity but uneven benefits.

The first round of jihads in the Western Sudan did not produce very formidable states. They have wider significance not only as precedents (and in some cases, bases) for later, more important movements but also because they reveal more immediately the impact of the new Atlantic economic frontier on West African societies already linked to the Sahara. Such a connection is most evident in the least successful of these movements, the Shurbubba (War of Bubba), which occurred between 1673 and 1677 among the Arabized Berber community of clergy and merchants in southwest Mauritania, a meeting point of Saharan and Atlantic commerce.

Nasir ad-Din, the Berber clerical leader of the Shurbubba, did not oppose the Atlantic slave trade explicitly. However, he directed his first attack against black rulers in neighboring Senegal who supplied slaves, including the forbidden category of Muslims, to Europeans. (Ironically, Bubba, in whose name the conflict began, was a Berber refugee from Nasir-ad-Din's own authority.) The Shurbubba enjoyed a few years of success but was soon crushed from two sides: Senegalese rulers, supported by their French slaving partners, and Arab warrior tribes, who claimed the right to political authority in Mauritania.

The three clerical states of Bundu, Futa Jallon, and Futa Toro founded in Senegal and Guinea between 1698 and 1776 better fit the model of later and larger jihads. In all these cases, the uprisings drew support from pastoral Fulani or Tukulor (a people who spoke the same language as the Fulani but mixed cattle-keeping with agriculture). A widening market economy gave pastoral groups opportunities to increase their wealth, and allowed some individuals to settle in urban areas and take up Islamic learning. Fulani and Tukulor Muslim scholars could thus become the leaders of communities who identified themselves both religiously and ethnically in opposition to the lack of Islamic orthodoxy among Mande agriculturalist rulers. The Futa Toro jihad at the end of the eighteenth century does not entirely fit this pattern, since the rulers on this Senegal-Mauritania borderland were already Fulani, though not clerics. But the real power here, as in the case of the Shurbubba, which was well known to Futa Toro Muslim scholars, lay in the hands of neighboring Arab warrior tribes. The jihadist could thus challenge existing authorities on both religious and ethnic grounds.

The new Sudanic clerical regimes took on more imperial dimensions in Sudanic regions closer to the major centers of trans-Saharan trade in the Middle Niger, the Hausa cities of Northern Nigeria, and the Lake Chad basin. The first of these powerful jihadist states in the Western Sudan emerged at the center of the Niger Delta among the Fulani of Masina. Its founder and longtime ruler, Sheikh Amadu Lobbo, was far less learned and much closer to Fulani pastoral life than most of the other jihad leaders. He is described, somewhat condescendingly, in the letter of a contemporary Timbuktu scholar as a man who "by his modesty succeeded in dominating the blacks and the whites, the learned and the warriors of his era."[9] Yet Amadu Lobbo managed to create the most orthodox theocratic government of the entire Sudan.

Masina, in the early 1800s, was already dominated by Fulani pastoralists, although their *ardos* (chiefs) held power as subordinates of the Bambara Segu Empire. No very strong scholarly tradition had developed in this community, and the local center of learning, Jenne—still under the nominal sovereignty of the Timbuktu Arma—was dominated by Berber, Sonrai, and Mande lineages more reputed for mutual power struggles than devotion to Islam. Amadu Lobbo, as a young student from a rural Fulani community, first suffered disdain from the Jenne elite. He later founded his own community just outside the city, only to be driven away as a threat to the local establishment. During the same period, word (in both written and oral form) filtered into Masina of a successful Fulani jihad farther to the east in Nigeria. In 1817, Amadu Lobbo offered his loyalty to the leader of this new state, Usman dan Fodio, in return for a commission to extend the movement to his own country. Soon after, responding to provocations from the local ardo, Amadu began his own jihad.

Within a few years, Amadu had secured political control of Masina and built in the savannah, away from the river, a new capital, Hamdullahi ("Praise God"). The eventual extent of this empire stretched over the entire Middle Niger, from just above Segu to just outside Timbuktu. Its population lived under very strict Islamic regulations, a condition reflecting Amadu Lobbo's limited interest in long-distance trade reaching toward either North Africa or the Atlantic. The core area of Masina, with its mixed pastoral, agricultural, and fishing economy, was largely self-sufficient. Even the vital military asset of horses could be raised locally, leaving salt as the only critical import. However, the regime depended heavily on the personal force of its founder, and after his death in 1845, Islamic fervor proved difficult to maintain. The Masina Caliphate would soon fall to a new Islamic power, more fresh in its jihadist dynamism and better equipped with imported firearms.

Al Hajj Umar Tal, the conqueror of both Segu and Masina, is unique among the jihad leaders of West Africa in his linking of virtually all the local traditions of holy war and his close ties to North Africa and the Middle East. Umar was born in the mid-1790s to a Tukulor clerical family in Futa Toro, an eighteenth-century jihadist state tied to the Shurbubba uprising of a century earlier. By Umar's time, Futa Toro's Islamic energies had waned, and it came under the political domination of Kaarta, an offshoot of the "pagan" Segu Empire. In the mid-1820s, he set off on a hajj (pilgrimage) to Mecca, making him the only regional jihadist to earn the title "Al Hajj." On his way back to his homeland, he spent extensive periods of time with the rulers of already established clerical states in the Central and Western Sudan, including Hamdullahi, the Masina capital. Umar's final place as guest cleric was Futa Jallon, a small-scale eighteenth century jihadist state in the Guinée highlands, where he had earlier studied.

In Futa Jallon, Umar first began to build up a large body of committed and well-armed followers, mostly Fulani and Tukulor from his home region of Futa Toro. Understandably, such a presence disturbed the Futa Jallon rulers, and Umar was encouraged to move into the small neighboring Mande (and thus "pagan") state of Tamba. When in turn the Tamba chief sent forces to disarm the clerical community, Umar not only felt politically justified in defending himself but also told a Moroccan biographer that "God Most High instructed me after the evening prayer.... In a great cry He said to me [three times] 'You are authorized to wage jihad in the name of Allah.'" [10]

The year was 1852, and Umar's forces not only defeated Tamba but went on to take Kaarta in 1855, Segu in 1861, and Masina in 1862. This last war between two jihadist states was costly in a number of ways. Amadu Lobo's successors counterattacked, killing Umar in 1864.

At its high point, Umar's empire extended over a wider area than even Segu had achieved. However, the new state was more proficient in warfare than in peacetime administration. After Umar's death, his sons and nephews disputed the succession and in effect established three separate capitals in Segu, Bandiagara (Masina), and Nioro (the old Kaarta center). When French colonial forces began their advance into the Middle Niger in the late 1880s, they picked off these towns in successive order, thus ending Islamic rule in this frontier of the Sahara.

In contrast to the Western Sudan, the political history of the Central Sudan and its neighboring desert zones is marked not by a succession of regional empires but rather parallel developments among two ethnic groups, the Kanuri and the Hausa. The Kanuri were the first of these two peoples to engage in trans-Saharan trade, and they produced a series of large-scale states, first in Kanem, a desert region to the north of Lake Chad, and then in Borno, to its south. The Kanem state emerged some time in the eighth century among black nomadic populations who had long been in contact with both agricultural regions of the Sudan and the central Saharan trading centers of Kawar. The Kanuri and related groups may have been victims of chariot-based slave raids from the Garamantes to their north. Very early in the Islamic era, however, the first rulers of Kanem, the Zaghawa, initiated a much larger slave trade under their own control.

Historians know little about the Zaghawa, not even what language they used. But in the ninth century, they were displaced by a new

Kanuri-speaking dynasty that reigned, in various forms and places, for almost a thousand years and produced extensive chronicles of its history. During the first two centuries of power, these kings were known as Duguwa. In 1075, a member of a different branch of the family, Hume, took the throne, and his successors later claimed descent from an Arabian migrant, Saif dhu Yadzan. The dynasty is known from this time until its formal demise in 1846 as the Saifawas, although also retaining the Kanuri title *mai* (king).

Kanem remained the base of the Saifawas until the late fourteenth century. Under the greatest king of this era, Mai Dunama Dibalami (1210–48)—"well known" (according to the thirteenth century North African geographer Ali ibn Musa Ibn Said) "for his religious warfare and charitable acts"[11]—the dynasty extended its rule as far north as the Fazzan. But in the following century, the Saifawas began to lose control of Kanem itself to other nomadic groups, including newly arrived Arab tribes. Even the capital of the monarchy, Njimi, became insecure due to invasions, succession struggles within the royal dynasty, and a desert ecology that could not support a growing urban population. Mai Umar ibn Idris (1382–87) is said in the royal chronicles to have consulted local Muslim scholars about his situation and received the answer "Leave this place, and the invader will vanish."[12]

It required almost a century for the Saifawas—under Mai Ali ibn Dunami, "the Conqueror" (1465–75)—to take full control of this savannah territory and establish themselves in a new capital, Birni Ngazargamo. During the following centuries, the Saifawas of Borno built perhaps the most powerful state of pre-nineteenth-century West and Central Africa. The lengthy reign of Mai Idris Alauma (1564–96) is particularly well known because a Kanuri Muslim scholar attached to his court, Ahmad ibn Fartu, recorded extensive accounts of "the military expeditions of our sultan and what he accomplished in the time of his reign, whether raids, holy war, defensive measures or making the highway safe for travelers." Most of these campaigns took place within the Sudan, but Mai Idris Alauma also attacked "the Tuareg, the marauders of the desert," not resting "until he had cast them into the pit of remorse, and given rest to the Muslims in the shade of ease and security."[13]

Such northward campaigns were needed because trans-Saharan links played a major role in Borno's success, not only as a source of commercial income but also in establishing diplomatic relations with North African regimes. Idris Alauma ruled during a period of intense international rivalry for control of the Maghrib. In search of military assistance for their own projects, the Borno rulers of this era offered their allegiance to both al-Mansur of Morocco and the sultan of the Ottoman Empire in Istanbul, who now controlled the coasts of Libya, Tunisia, and Algeria, as well as the Saharan region of Fazzan. No formal alliance was ever established with either of these powers, but Borno did receive firearms and advice in their use from the sultan's representative in Tripoli. Thus the Kanuri state strengthened its capacity for local control just at the time the Songhay Empire was falling victim to the same military technology.

In the early nineteenth century a Fulani jihadist cleric, Usman dan Fodio, attacked the Saifawas from Hausaland and brought about the demise of the dynasty—but not of Borno. The Borno kings of this period proved unequal to the challenge and turned to the Sahara for help. The savior of Borno was a Muslim scholar, Muhammad al-Amin al-Kanemi, born in the Fazzan to a Kanem father and an Arab mother. Although maintaining the clerical title "Shehu," al-Kanemi did not attempt any major religious reform in the already highly Islamized Borno but took practical charge of the regime. He left the Saifawa kings nominally in office but set up an alternate capital at Kukawa in 1814. Using his own African and Arab military forces from Kanem and the Fazzan, he defended Borno against the Fulani, extended its boundaries to the south, and reestablished internal control.

At Muhammad al-Kanemi's death, his son and successor, Umar (1837–81), eliminated the last of the Saifawa rulers, thus formalizing the shift to a new Shehu dynasty. The resulting combination of Sudanic, Saharan, and Islamic political culture was observed in 1871 by the German explorer Gustav Nachtigal. He describes a royal court that now reproduced the elaborate ranks and protocols of the defunct Saifawas but had at its center a ruler whose entire appearance was "that of a well-to-do man of Fazzan, with a simplicity of clothing and adornment reminding us of his religious character."[14]

Hausaland was always one of the wealthiest and most densely populated regions in the entire Sudanic belt, but it entered relatively late into the system of trans-Saharan commerce. Moreover, until the 1800s, Hausa political history consisted of rivalries, in various combinations, among the more powerful local city-states (Kano, Katsina, Zaria, Kebbi, and Gobir) or incursions from the surrounding empires of Songhay and Borno. Beginning in the 1500s, Songhay and Borno also contended with Hausa states for influence over the Saharan gateway to the region's cross-desert trade, the Tuareg sultanate of Agades in Ahir. These conflicts did not undermine the increasing prosperity

Muhammad al-Amin al-Kanemi became ruler of the Sudanic Borno Empire in 1814, displacing the nine-hundred-year-old Saifawa dynasty. Like the jihadist leaders of the Sokoto Caliphate, whose attacks he successfully fended off, al-Kanemi was a Muslim scholar before he assumed political power. Source: Dixon Denham and Hugh Clapperton, Narrative of Travels and Discoveries in Northern and Central Africa, in the Years 1822, 1823, and 1824 *(1824).* Courtesy Joseph Regenstein Library, University of Chicago of Hausaland, which benefited from both trans-Saharan and Atlantic trade. However, the region now became vulnerable to aggression not only from outside but also, and more fatally, from alienated insiders.

These internal conquerors were Fulani, mobilized into religious war by one of their own scholars, Usman dan Fodio. As elsewhere in the Western and Central Sudan, the Fulani of Hausaland had prospered from the growing trade of the region but also suffered from continuous local warfare. Much of Usman's public preaching, which began in his native Gobir in the mid 1770s, simply asked Hausaland residents who already called themselves Muslims to follow their faith more seriously. But these appeals soon transformed into attacks on rulers who, as described by Usman's son and key supporter, Muhammad Bello, "knew not the [Islamic] Law thoroughly. And as for their judgments they followed the practices of their fathers who knew not Mohammedanism." Shortly after he began his jihad, Usman himself published his *Kitab al-Farq* (Book of Differences), which catalogues at great length "the ways of unbelievers in their governments." These include the usual list of illegal taxes, but special mention is made of the *janghali*, a requisition of cattle that fell particularly hard on Fulani herders and even urban scholars who depended on this form of easily transferred wealth. Another charge against the Hausa kings was their continual hunting for slaves, even among free Muslims. In a pre-jihad poem Usman had warned: "And one who enslaves a freeman.... The Fire shall enslave him."[15]

Usman originally hoped that Yunfa, the ruler of his home state, Gobir, would cooperate in achieving more orthodox religious practice and social justice. However, the commitment of the Hausa kings to local rituals and the necessities of state power eventually led Yunfa instead to put prohibitions on Usman's public activities, which the latter in turn denounced as direct attacks against Islam. Usman then followed the model of the Prophet Muhammad during his own quarrels with the elites of Mecca and went into *hijra* (flight) from the center of Gobir to Degal, a rural settlement under his own control. The actual jihad began in 1804, when Yunfa's forces attacked Degal. The followers of Usman were now strong enough to fight back and within four years had conquered Gobir and established a new regional capital at Sokoto.

During the first phase of his uprising, Usman attracted followers from a wide range of social-ethnic groups, including not only Fulani herders but also Hausa farmers and Tuareg nomads. As the movement expanded beyond Gobir, however, it based itself increasingly on Fulanis, who served as both scholarly commanders (emirs) in various regions and as a pastoralist military base. In some Hausa kingdoms as well as in Borno and even Masina, would-be emirs came to Sokoto to receive banners licensing them to fight their own campaigns in the name of the Sokoto caliph (first Usman and then Muhammad Bello).

The new Sokoto Caliphate extended, by the late 1830s, over almost all of Hausaland plus several important areas to the east and south, such as Adamawa in present-day Cameroon, along with the Bauchi Plateau, Nupe, and Ilorin in Nigeria. Each of the emirates making up the empire became a hereditary rulership of its own, following many of the precedents (and language) of earlier well-developed Hausa states; but the whole structure maintained a degree of central coordination well beyond that of previous Sudanic empires. Even after its defeat by British forces in 1903, the Sokoto regime survived, along with the Shehus of Borno, as a basis for British administration in colonial Nigeria.

The narratives of rising and falling states across the different zones touched by trans-Saharan trade provides a history focused on the rulers of the desert and its shores. It does not tell us very much about how these regimes attempted to control the lands—often very vast—and populations to which they laid claim. Were these territories clearly defined? Did their inhabitants identify with or participate in their central governments? What legal systems and instruments of power were employed to maintain order? What services did states provide to their populations?

In 1824, Muhammad Bello, then ruler of the Sokoto Caliphate, drew a map of his domains at the request of a European explorer. The result gives a reasonably accurate idea of how far his authority extended but also an indication of the limits of that power. In the first place, Muhammad Bello, a highly literate Muslim scholar, did not feel the need to make such maps for his own purposes, nor did he have any written lists of the populations under Sokoto sovereignty. His map provides good information on the issues that most mattered to the Sokoto Caliphate: the capital city and its immediate surroundings, the major Hausa cities it controlled, and the trade routes toward the Sahara and the Atlantic Ocean. What it lacks are precisely drawn and agreed-upon boundaries. Instead, the caliphate had frontiers, that is, zones where its power came into conflict with other groups who might either challenge its sovereignty or be raided for slaves and other booty.

Sokoto was one of the most developed of the Sudanic empires, so the way it represented its territory can be seen as typical of, if not superior to, such capacities among governments throughout this region. North Africa had a longer history of centralized rule and use of writing than the Sudan, but there, too, no governments had drawn maps of the lands they ruled. The closest approximation came in the 1500s,

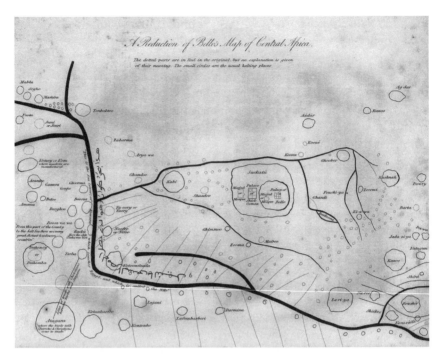

Muhammad Bello, ruler of the Sokoto Caliphate, drew this map in 1824 at the instigation of the European explorer Hugh Clapperton. It indicates a large empire with strategic bases along key trade routes but no clear territorial boundaries.
Source: Dixon Denham and Hugh Clapperton, Narrative of Travels and Discoveries in Northern and Central Africa, in the Years 1822, 1823, and 1824 (1824). Courtesy Joseph Regenstein Library, University of Chicago

when the Ottoman Empire took over the eastern and central Maghrib coastal zones and, following its established Middle East practices, sent out bureaucrats to make tax surveys of the hinterland population. The resulting lists (without maps) were not, however, revised until the eve of colonization in the 1800s.

If the territorial shape of states bordering the Sahara (to say nothing of those within it) remained somewhat vague, the populations inhabiting them also lacked a common cultural identity. In North Africa and the Sahara, Arabic did become widespread, in both spoken and written form, but very large populations still spoke (but rarely wrote) Berber languages. The Sudanic empires were even more linguistically divided and seldom used writing for any secular purposes.

Islam did provide some basis for unity throughout the region and, in the Sahara and Sudan, also inspired the beginning of writing in indigenous African languages. It also propagated a legal system known as the Shariah, which states could potentially use to make rule over wide areas more uniform and legitimate. The various jihads in the Sudan and even the initial Arab conquest of North Africa justified themselves by claiming the goal of such a religiously based code for society. However, even the most sincere efforts at Islamic legal reform remained incomplete, confined mainly to urban areas that accounted for only a small minority of the North and West African populations. Rural areas experienced their own contacts with Islam, but these came through the presence of merchants and scholars rather than state representatives.

In any case, Islamic rules did not cover every issue of concern to governments and sometimes, especially in the area of taxation, imposed impractical restrictions upon rulers. All Muslim regimes thus recognized some legal practices already in place among communities under their control, as well as government arbitration that lay outside the Shariah. The Ottoman regime created a separate system of formal administrative law, called *qanun*, which regulated most government operations, but its jurisdiction did not extend very far into Africa.

Because they did not follow a clearly defined system of law or represent the interests of their populations either through appeals to ethnic identity or by establishing elected legislatures, the precolonial regimes of Africa are often referred to as "despotisms." Many actions of rulers in these regions may seem arbitrary and cruel to us, particularly when they fought one another for power or enslaved neighboring populations. However, most of their subjects did not feel oppressed by their governments, or at least the government at the center of the state. In many rural areas, communities of farmers and herders even enjoyed a kind of "democracy" in which most decisions were made by councils of the male heads of households. Such systems excluded many adults from public life, including men without families, women, and slaves. But even these groups often found indirect ways of exerting influence, and at least the free males (and some slaves) could nourish hopes for obtaining fuller rights at some later stage in their own lives or those of their children. Even where "aristocrats" of various kinds had control over the property and labor of local populations, these forces balanced local interests against those of the central regime.

There were thus two kinds of restriction on the kings and emperors of Northern Africa and the Sudan. First, the long-established governing systems of households, villages, nomadic tribes, and even local chiefdoms acted as a kind of unwritten constitution that central rulers could not easily violate. Second, the instruments of executive power available to central rulers in this part of the world were weak.

As much as we might like to think otherwise, the main business of most governments in world history, including those around the Sahara, has been warfare. Rulers here not only had to protect themselves against rivals but also to defend their populations from the kind of raids that they themselves undertook against neighboring zones. Such marauding also provided one of the major sources of public revenue. Even in North Africa, where black slaves were mainly purchased from trans-Saharan merchants rather than captured directly, local regimes launched pirate vessels (the notorious Barbary corsairs) into the Mediterranean for the purpose of seizing not only cargoes but also European crews and passengers. One of the functions of these white slaves was military service, and they made up the majority of the Moroccan army that conquered Songhay in the 1590s.

As recounted here so far, the successes and failures of the various regimes that contended for power around the Sahara seemed to depended on the skill and courage of individual leaders and, sometimes, religious fervor. These are important factors, but historians also need to consider the more impersonal and secular issues of military technology and the recruitment of reliable troops. The two resources are closely linked, as the materials used to fight determined how armies were organized and even what kind of economic support they needed. The easiest place to begin describing them is with the "hardware" of war.

In the initial Arab conquest of North Africa and the rise of Sudanic empires from at least the thirteenth century, weapons were less important to armies than transportation—more specifically, horses. If camels made possible the commercial and political mastery of the Sahara itself, horses decided who would rule the zones connected by cross-desert trade. The largest part of most state armies still consisted of foot soldiers, but horses gave armies decisive mobility over wide areas and within battlefields. Villagers targeted by slavers could do little to defend themselves against cavalry raids, despite the widespread presence of bows and arrows (often tipped with poison) that might wound or kill horses. The rise of the Segu state does show that some villagers could organize themselves against these raids, but this was generally difficult in dispersed and small rural communities. Moreover, for protection against arrows, horsemen in at least the Central Sudan often covered themselves and their mounts with elaborate armor made of leather, imported metal, or quilted cotton.

From the 1400s onward, Europe and the Middle East experienced a "gunpowder revolution" in which the supremacy of cavalries was challenged by infantry units bearing firearms and fighting in close formations that also made use of pikes or bayonets. Such armies were able to repel the charges of horsemen, who now become relegated to a secondary, if still glamorous, role in warfare. Cavalry had been associated with decentralized political organization, in which aristocratic classes maintained horses and developed the skills to use them on their own lands. The new infantry-centered armies had to be organized, trained, and paid by central governments, and this effort required increased public revenues. Historians of early modern Europe see the new style of warfare as an important element in the simultaneous development of powerful states and more productive economies.

In the Islamic world, the Ottoman Empire took up the gunpowder challenge with great energy and reorganized its military forces around a musket-bearing infantry, the famed janissaries (from Turkish *yeni,* meaning "new, modern," and *tsheri,* meaning "army"). These armies allowed the Ottomans to conquer Egypt in 1517 and then advance into North Africa. The Moroccan rulers of this era also built their armies around firearms and used the new formations to fight off both the Ottomans and Portuguese in North Africa and Songhay in the trans-Saharan expedition of 1591.

Ibn Fartu's chronicle of sixteenth-century Borno lists among the glories of Mai Idris Alauma "the Turkish musketeers present with him and the great number of slaves of foreign origin who were trained and skilled in the use of muskets."[16] But the same account indicates how little impact such weapons had on either warfare or state organization. To begin with, cavalry warfare had never been as decentralized here as in Europe and the Middle East, because horses had to be imported through urban markets or bred in a few favored areas such as the Niger Delta, rather than raised on the rural estates of warrior elites. But the main reason neither the new guns nor the old bows made little difference has to do with the nature of Sudanic warfare or, to put it another way, the purposes for which states employed their armies.

Pitched encounters between massed armies of rival states seldom occurred in the Sudan. Few regimes here could raise large armies, and military expeditions were usually raids, either to ward off threats and collect revenue or (more commonly) to capture slaves. The victims of such attacks did not employ massed infantry tactics because, in scattered villages, they could not or because they had their own means of mobility, especially in the Sahara. City-dwellers in the Sudan used the clay walls surrounding their towns as defenses, and these could withstand all but the most sustained sieges until artillery arrived, usually with European colonial forces.

Panzerreiter in Bornû.

A warrior of the Borno Empire and his horse are both clad in armor made from quilted cotton. This combination of mobility and protection allowed the regimes of the Central Sudan to capture slaves from among rural populations whose main weapons were bows and arrows. Source: Gustav Nachtigal, Sahărâ und Sûdân: Ergebnisse sechsjähriger Reisen in Afrika, *(1879), 1. Courtesy Joseph Regenstein Library, University of Chicago*

One well-documented instance exists of a Sudanic military victory that is explained by the inadvertent use of "revolutionary" tight formation tactics. In 1804, Yunfa, the Hausa ruler of Gobir, attacked the lightly armed followers of Usman dan Fodio's jihad with what appeared to be an overwhelmingly superior force, mounted on horses and camels and even bearing a few muskets. According to Muhammad Bello's biography of his father, the jihadists prevailed because "God broke the army of the heathen."[17] A more secular explanation to be drawn from the details of the same eyewitness account is that after the enemy broke the outer wings of their battle formation, Usman's army was forced to bunch into close ranks at its center. These formations could not be penetrated by the Gobir cavalry charges and in turn released concentrated archery volleys on the attackers, eventually dispersing them. Such events repeated themselves in several later battles of the jihad, but these tactics were abandoned once the new Sokoto Empire itself became a horse-based, slave-raiding regime.

Guns did make a difference at the battle of Tondibi, but the Moroccan forces employed tactics developed during earlier gunpowder warfare in North Africa against a Songhay enemy with no such experience. Even so, most accounts describe the encounter as taking a good deal more than "the twinkling of an eye," and firearms did little to strengthen the Arma regime that took over the Middle Niger from Songhay. The Segu Empire of the late 1700s and early 1800s had plenty of muskets and organized its own production of gunpowder among fishing populations along the Niger River. But the guns themselves had to be imported via either the Sahara or the Atlantic in exchange for slaves, and to procure these, Segu used horse-borne raids rather than massed infantry.

In the last half of the nineteenth century, more efficient firearms began to enter the Sahara and Sudan, although they did not change military tactics or political and social organization. The jihadist armies of Al Hajj Umar Tal conquered Segu in 1861 with the aid of double-barreled muskets that could be fired directly from horseback. By the end of the century, more and better versions of these weapons (along with the artillery that was also used by the Umarians) arrived in the region under the control of European colonial armies, who put an end to indigenous projects of state-building.

Much of what might be considered the "civilian" aspects of Maghrib and Sudanic governments was closely linked to military needs. In their early conquering stages, many of these regimes organized their forces around existing kinship groups of pastoral peoples: the tribes of the early Arab invaders of North Africa as well as the clans of various

Fulani groups in the Sudan and Berbers and Arabs in the Sahara. The major income of such groups came from booty, but they can be considered states rather than simply marauders (like the later Hilali and Sulaim Arab invaders of the Maghrib) as long as they supported a central authority. Islamic law in fact specifies that one-fifth of all wealth seized in warfare must go to the ruler.

Once conquest ended, it was difficult to maintain order on this basis. Kin units had their own leaders who might revolt or at least resist paying taxes to a ruler who had no independent means of dominating them. In the desert, the Sahel, or the mountainous regions of the Maghrib and the Sudanic states, tribal systems survived into the colonial era. States to the north or south of the Sahara sometimes established their own military-administrative bases in key centers of desert trade or salt mining such as Awdaghust, Taghaza, and the Fazzan, but this kind of control never lasted very long. Regimes centered in Saharan oases and highlands such as Murzuk or Agades were more stable, although modest in their territorial ambitions. In most of the desert as well as the steppe and mountain hinterlands of North Africa, "rule" was exercised through periodic expeditions in which state forces joined with local allies to collect taxes from other groups or at least keep them under restraint.

Agricultural populations in both the Maghrib and Sudan were more easily subjugated and provided many of the foot soldiers for state armies as well as the tax revenue to support mounted military forces. Most of the central governments in these regions did not administer rural areas directly but assigned them as estates to the leaders of their armies. Under the most effective regimes, such as Borno, these lands not only supported their "lords" but also paid taxes (in the form of both foodstuffs and money) to the central ruler. If the estate holders proved disloyal or ineffective, they could, in principle, be removed. However, the ability of rulers to exert such authority varied considerably, according to both their individual abilities and the availability of instruments other than personal loyalty to control outlying territories. The most common of these instruments was a military force independent of the state's aristocrats.

In both North Africa and the Sudan, rulers created these armies by recruiting slave soldiers. In the Maghrib, the slaves used for military purposes were most often racially distinct black Africans or white Europeans and Central Asians, including the Ottoman janissaries. But this was not true in the Sudan, where both slaves and masters were black. The servile troops on both sides of the Sahara were primarily defined as outsiders, men who had no allegiances or kin ties within the societies where they served other than to the rulers who employed them. In some cases, the outside forces might even be voluntary "mercenaries," as were some Spanish Christians in the Moroccan force that invaded the Sudan and Turkish musketeers in the Borno armies.

In time, of course, even slave military groups developed collective social identities of their own. Sometimes these groups seized power and became new ruling dynasties (like the Jara of Segu and possibly the Askias of Songhay) or became "tribes" with assigned local territories (as did the black army of the Alawite regime in eighteenth-century Morocco). Their royal masters needed to manage them skillfully in order to retain their loyalty, and some kind of taxation was necessary for their support. The latter condition became particularly important after the gunpowder revolution, when weapons had to be paid for in cash and skilled infantry, even if recruited as slaves, required payment and supplies.

Slave armies partially provided their own income, insofar as they helped rulers raid outside areas or extract tribute from them. Within the frontiers of the state, they also enforced tax collection in herding and agricultural regions administered by locally based aristocrats. However, if governments in this region were to remain stable over long periods of time, they also needed revenue sources that did not depend so heavily on violence. They achieved these goals, at least partially, through the control of markets and the management of more general affairs by a civilian bureaucracy. Markets provided one of the most accessible sources of income for rulers because they were centered in the urban areas directly under their control. Governments could thus collect taxes on such ordinary transactions as the importation of produce into cities and its local sale.

Foreign commerce was even more valuable to both Maghrib and Sudanic states, both as direct participants and collectors of tax revenue. The immediate role of states in trade, again, depended on violence. In the Sudan, the one export commodity supplied by government agents was slaves, whom they captured through warfare. From the early 1500s, Maghrib regimes derived a considerable portion of their income from piracy and the resulting ransom of European captives. In both regions, however, most external commerce took place between private merchants in commodities derived from more peaceful activities such as mining, agriculture, and herding. Foreign buyers of these goods established privileged relationships with local rulers, receiving their protection and the right to their own jurisdiction (Muslim in the Sudan, Christian and Jewish in the Maghrib) in return for financial support of various kinds. But in this case, too, the states based their powers on relationships remote from the normal lives of their subjects.

North African and Sudanic governments could not expect much involvement by the general populations under their rule, as they offered these communities—especially in rural areas—few services other than a somewhat ambivalent protection against violence. Throughout the premodern Islamic world—as in Europe until at least the late Middle Ages—many activities associated with modern states, such as education and care for the sick and poor, were undertaken by religious bodies rather than government agencies. Islamic clergy, under varying degrees of state control, also carried out most judicial functions and supervised markets. The literacy and administrative skills fostered by Muslim clerical education could (again as in medieval Europe) provide training for men to serve as viziers (ministers) and scribes in the management of the state. However, such government bureaucracies as existed in trans-Saharan Africa concerned themselves with matters of more interest to the government itself than to the public.

Foremost among these interests was, of course, taxation. Officials took responsibility for collecting, guarding, and paying out government monies as well as, in the most ambitious case, undertaking investigations of the potential sources for such revenue. Few regimes, even in the more literate Maghrib, actually managed long-term record-keeping. In 1159, Abd-al-Mumin, caliph of the Almohades, the last regime to rule over a united North Africa, proposed a revenue survey of his eastern domains; but this undertaking never got past the planning stage. The Ottomans did produce such a document for the same region four centuries later, but could not keep it up to date afterward. The main object of both these efforts was Tunisia, whose wheat and olive crops had so enriched Carthage and Rome. However even here the local bey had, by the late 1700s, sold rural revenue collection offices to the highest bidders, thus abandoning any direct responsibility for taxation.

Government scribes in North Africa and the most developed Sudanic states such as the Sokoto Caliphate did keep some records of income received and also corresponded with subordinate officials. In most of the Sahara and Sudan, such official writing was confined to chronicles of rulers' lives and letters to foreign rulers. As early as 1391, one such message arrived in Cairo from a contemporary ruler of Borno pleading (in vain, as it turned out) for "the mighty king of Egypt" to dispatch his "emirs, ministers, judges, magistrates, jurists, [and] market overseers" to find some of his subjects who had been illegally enslaved by Saharan Arabs and "restore them to their freedom and Islam."[18]

Even the records maintained by the viziers of nineteenth-century Sokoto address what we might think of as diplomatic relations within the caliphate rather than the daily business of governance. Thus we find the sultan Muhammad Bello informing a subordinate emir of a forthcoming frontier expedition in which he expects "those of the brethren who adjoin us to follow us and to march out with us, bring their beasts and military equipment."[19] Other letters address boundary disputes among the emirates, succession disputes within them, and (quite frequently) runaway slaves. The vizier often traveled to various emirates and attempted to arbitrate disputes there, but the details of these cases were left to local officials who were not required to provide written reports of their actions.

The political history of trans-Saharan Africa is rich in the drama of conflicts and personalities, yet somewhat disappointing with regard to how civil governments operated and what they did for their populations. But both the glory and limitations of these states left much room for the economic, religious, and cultural aspects of desert exchanges to flourish on their own.

CHAPTER 4

Islam

T he city of Ghana," the eleventh-century Arab geographer Abu
Ubayd Abd Allah al-Bakri reports, "consists of two towns....One,
inhabited by Muslims, is large and has twelve mosques" along
with various kinds of Islamic officials and clergy. "The king's town is
six miles distant" and contains, among other features, "the sorcerers of
these people, men in charge of the religious cult," as well as "their idols
and the tombs of their kings."[1]

Al-Bakri describes a middle phase in the religious transformation
of trans-Saharan Africa, one historians often refer to as the "spread
of Muslims" rather than the "spread of Islam." For the urban-based
North African merchants who crossed the desert to live in the first of
al-Bakri's two towns, Islam was already a well-developed religious and
even professional identity. The king of Ghana and his people traded
regularly with these Muslims but remained unconverted to their faith.
In the succeeding centuries, Islam would penetrate much more deeply
into the commercial and political life of Saharan and Sudanic society
and spread beyond it, carried by savannah-based merchants into the
forest zones of West Africa.

Islam is one of the world's most widespread and dynamic faiths,
with a complex set of beliefs and practices. However, according to the
credo of the fifteenth-century theologian Muhammad ibn Yusuf al-
Sanusi, the most frequently cited source on correct Muslim belief in
trans-Saharan Africa, "all that which it is incumbent upon the legally
responsible person to know of the articles of faith concerning the Most
High and concerning His prophets" is "the two words of testimony,"
which are known as the Shahadah: "There is no god but Allah and
Muhammad is the Messenger of Allah."[2]

The first part of this avowal indicates that Islam is a monotheistic
religion, descended from Judaism and Christianity. By contrast, the traditional belief systems of Mediterranean and especially tropical Africa
directed their worship at a multiplicity of spiritual forces emanating
from the natural world and various ancestors. The prophetic role of
Muhammad identifies Islam with a specific time and place: the early
seventh century CE in the west Arabian city of Mecca (622, the date of

Muhammad's Hijra [emigration] from Mecca, is the first year of the Muslim calendar). Islam respects the divine messages contained in the Jewish and Christian Bibles, but Muhammad is the "seal of the prophets," meaning that after him there can be no further systematic revelations from God. At the same time, Muhammad is a historical human being who provides a model that can be emulated by later Muslim figures, especially those who claim, either through inheritance or personal charisma, the power to combine religious and political leadership.

The Shahadah is one of the "five pillars" of Islam, along with prayer, the giving of alms, daytime fasting during the holy month of Ramadan, and (when possible) pilgrimage (hajj) to Mecca. The last of these requirements provided an important motive for travel across the Sahara. Pilgrims not only fulfilled a personal obligation but also kept Muslims from all regions of Africa in contact with the centers of their faith, both in Mecca and the Mediterranean stopping places on the way to Arabia.

Islam is a religion based on written books. This again links it to Judaism and Christianity, whose practitioners are respected by Muslims as Ahl-al-Kitab (People of the Book), and contrasts with the orally based traditions of tropical Africa. The teachings of Islamic scripture are closer to those of Judaism than Christianity because they stress not only belief, ritual, and general morality but also specific regulations of daily life in the home, the marketplace, and affairs of state. Ibn Battuta, the fourteenth-century Muslim visitor to the court of Mali, was appalled to see that "their women go into the sultan's presence naked" and "many of them eat carrion, and dogs and donkeys."[3]

Islamic religious texts are not accessible to most believers. They require not only literacy but also knowledge of a form of Arabic that differs from local dialects of the language that people (especially North Africans) use in their daily lives. Most Muslims, especially in urban areas, study the most holy of these books, the Quran (containing Allah's original revelation to Muhammad); but they do so by rote in order to familiarize themselves with the phrases used in prayer rather than to develop the ability to read other texts, especially if they do not know Arabic. This practice is very similar to the traditional use of Latin and Hebrew by Catholics and Jews who did not speak these sacred languages. Eventually, concern for the propagation and reform of religion led, as in Europe, to translations of sacred texts into indigenous African languages of both the Sahara and Sudan.

The teaching and study of the Quran, the Hadith (records of the subsequent words and actions of the Prophet), and the many secondary works based on these sources depended on a specially trained group of scholars, the ulama (people of *ilm*, religious learning), who are often referred to as a clergy. Islam does not recognize any priesthood, that is, men or women with sacred powers organized through something like a church. However, individuals who achieve an accepted standard of proficiency in the sacred texts take on a role which resembles that of Jewish rabbis or Protestant pastors. The ulama have a number of specific religious and social tasks. They lead prayers, teach both ordinary believers and more advanced students, carry on their own scholarly researches and writings, serve as *qadis* (judges) to interpret Shariah (religious law), and often provide help to the sick and poor.

Although the original model of Islam was that of a theocracy, with Muhammad as both prophet and ruler, in later Muslim societies religion became separate from the state. The degree to which rulers allowed the ulama independent jurisdiction over public matters varied considerably from regime to regime. Governments had the power to appoint qadis, but such men earned their qualifications through the study of a legal system that could, in principle, be evoked against the ruler. For some areas of public administration, rulers established a separate legal system outside the Shariah.

Taxes collected by the state were supposed to provide financial support for the ulama, but other sources were almost always available. In the Middle East, North Africa, and the Sahara, well-to-do individuals could deposit titles to land, urban buildings, or other bases of wealth in a *waqf* (religious foundation), which could function as a family trust but was often dedicated to funding mosques or other institutions under ulama control, such as schools, hospitals, or charities. Waqfs are seldom found in the Sudan because agricultural land in this region is generally not treated as private property and permanent private buildings are rare. However, rulers here often created independent sources of income for ulama by granting them authority over small rural territories and—more important—their inhabitants, without obligations to pay taxes on the resulting revenues.

In the North African interior and the Sahara, Muslim scholarship became integrated into a complex social hierarchy. At the top were nomadic tribes dedicated to warfare: descendants of Hilali Arab immigrants in much of the Maghrib hinterland and western Sahara, and *imashaghen* (noble) Tuareg in the central Sahara. Ulama belonged to religious settlements known as *marabouts* in the Maghrib, *zawiya* in the western Sahara, and *inesleman* among the Tuareg. They gave up violence and political power but might mediate between the warrior groups. More generally, they were guaranteed the protection of those in power, often in landscapes supporting relatively dense settlement, so that they could pursue the study of Islam along with a wide range of economic activities.

The zawiya in the western Sahara were mostly descended from Sanhaja Berbers who had been conquered and Arabized by a branch of the Hilali known as Hassani. It made some sense for Muslim scholars based in settlements with a long history of agriculture and trade to limit their political function to mediation. However, the failed Shurbubba revolt of the 1670s indicates the dissatisfaction of some zawiya leaders with this subordinate position, as well as the difficulty of reversing it.

The inesleman (Muslim) tribes of the central Sahara had a similarly restricted relationship to the local warrior groups but did not enjoy as great a status as the zawiya. Less is known about their degree of Islamic learning, perhaps because of their greater distance from both European and Arab sources of information. One obstacle to Islam in this region, in contrast with the western Sahara, was the commitment of its dominant Tuareg population to their own language, culture, and bedouin economy. The major scholarly efforts here first developed in regional trading centers such as Tadmakkat (also known as Es-Suq, "the Market") in the Adrar highlands and later at Agades and agricultural settlements in the surrounding Ahir Mountains. Other members of this scholarly community dispersed more widely throughout the Sahara, but the Berber-Arabic name they adopted, Kel-es-Suq (People of the Market), recalls their origin long after the collapse of Tadmakkat.

As was the case in Ahir, Muslim scholars could often earn a living without support from government or charitable foundations by providing legal and educational services, engaging in commerce, practicing specified handicrafts such as embroidery, and farming, using their own labor as well as that of their pupils and slaves. The world of Islamic learning was not only autonomous in this way but also extended well beyond the boundaries of specific states, regions, or even continents. Mediterranean ulama such as Ibn Battuta traveled throughout the Sahara and Sudan (and in the case of Ibn Battuta, also around the entire Indian Ocean). Likewise, African students and mature scholars regularly went north of the desert not only on pilgrimage to the holy sites of Arabia but also to stay at centers of learning in North Africa and Egypt (where special hostels were established to accommodate them). Some North African scholars also came to study in Sudanic mosque schools, such as those of Timbuktu. Even when travel was not possible, points of law or religious doctrine and practice could be pursued over wide distances by means of written correspondence in the universal medium of classical Arabic.

The Islamic faith has been divided from its earliest centuries into a number of competing sects, all of which made their appearance in Africa. The vast majority of Muslims would describe themselves as Sunni (orthodox), meaning that they accept the legitimacy of the caliphs (viceroys) who succeeded to the authority of Muhammad, first in Mecca and then in various major cites of the Middle East (Damascus, Baghdad, Cairo, Istanbul) and follow the four main schools of legal interpretation. The major dissenting sect, the Shia, claims loyalty to an alternate line of caliphs (or, in their terminology, imams) descended from Ali, the son-in-law of the Prophet through marriage to Muhammad's daughter, Fatima. At various times and places in Islamic history (including modern Iraq, Lebanon, and Pakistan) this allegiance has led to political conflicts with Sunnis. More enduringly, it produced a somewhat different set of Shariah interpretations and ritual practices. Another dissenting version of Islam with especially strong appeal in North Africa was Kharaj (secession). The Kharijites refused submission to any line of hereditary caliphs.

Originally, all these variations of Islam were mainly concerned with who should exercise political authority over the Muslim community. In time, however, the more established Sunni regimes developed the kinds of clerical institutions that could focus their attention on matters of doctrine and law without direct involvement in struggles over rulership. The Shiites and Kharijites, with their shared notion of the imam as both religious and political leader, continued for much longer to challenge the existing political order and, in turn, were held in suspicion by Sunni regimes.

North Africa is a good example of these tensions. For the first century and a half after its initial Muslim conquest, local governors acted as representatives of the Sunni Umayyad and Abbasid caliphs (based, successively, in Damascus and Baghdad). Even when the Aghlabid emirs set themselves up in 800 as a hereditary dynasty in the eastern Maghrib, they continued to give nominal support to the Baghdad caliphs. However, the Abbasid regime itself was still in a formative stage at this time and flirted with Shiism as well as Mutazalism, a new interpretation of Islam that drew heavily on Greek philosophy. During the early 800s Qayrawan, the Tunisian capital of the Aghlabids, became the site of a major religious controversy. On one side stood the rulers and their close followers, who championed the more intellectually sophisticated Baghdad tendencies; on the other were the local ulama, who favored a strict Sunni doctrine that could appeal to the Berber masses.

Two devotees are seated in the mihrab, or prayer niche, of the Sidi Boumediene mosque in Tlemcen, Algeria. The mosque and adjoining tomb of Sidi Boumediene, a twelfth-century teacher of Sufism, are the objects of pilgrimage from all over North Africa. Library of Congress, LC-DIG-ppmsca-04592

The ulama won out because they combined a strong position within the already venerable mosques of Qayrawan with an intellectual capacity to formulate the legal school of their choice, the strictly orthodox Malikism, into a coherent system. A key figure in all these efforts was the ninth-century Qayrawan scholar and qadi Sahnun ibn Said. Not only—in the words of the tenth-century historian Abu Bakr al-Maliki— "harsh against the people of innovations," Sahnun may also have been more important than the Arabian founder of Malikism, Malik ibn Anas, in establishing the main tendencies of this school. As one of his contemporaries, Amr ibn Yazid, stated, "If I had said that Sahnun had more *fiqh* [legal learning] than all the companions of Malik, I would be telling the truth."[4] Through these efforts, Qayrawan retained its position as the most powerful center for the teaching of orthodox Islamic theology and law in the Maghrib and eventually extended its influence into the Sahara and Sudan.

Sunni Islam met serious competition in North Africa from both Shiites and Kharijites. The earliest of these threats came in the form of Kharijism, which found support all over the region as a focus of Berber rebellion. During the mid-700s, Kharijites controlled not only the countryside but also Qayrawan, where extremist members of the Sufri sect desecrated the main mosque. By 771, forces loyal to the Abbasid Caliphate had regained control over the entire coastal region, restricting the Kharijites—now dominated by the more moderate Ibadi sect—to the interior. From the eighth to the early tenth centuries, the era of their independent Tahert state, the Ibadis remained a major political force in North Africa. However, their more lasting and significant impact came through the settlements on the edge of the Sahara, from where Ibadi merchants first spread Islam into the desert and the Sudan.

In the Maghrib, the Shia continued, often in very dramatic fashion, to challenge Sunni domination. The first major North African rulers to claim descent from Ali were the eighth-century Idrissids of Morocco. This dynasty never established very firm or wide-ranging political or Shia religious authority, but it did bring Islam to the "Far West" of the Muslim world. The two lasting monuments of the Idrissids, the city of Fez and the tomb of Idris I, embody the dual nature of North African faith. One is an urban center of Sunni Muslim learning (its main mosque is called al-Qayrawiyyin: People of Qayrawan); the other is the object of a more controversial Berber tendency to venerate local Muslim "saints."

The most sensational Shia eruption in this region, the rise of the Fatimid Caliphate, occurred as the result of a conspiracy throughout the Islamic world to replace the Abbasids with a descendant of Ismail, the seventh imam in line of succession from Ali. Ismaili propagandists succeeded, during the late 800s, in creating a military base out of a major mountain Berber tribe in the central Maghrib, the Kutama. In 910, this new force took over Tunisia from the independent Sunni regime of the Aghlabids. However, the main object of the Fatimids was always to control the core Middle East base of Islam. They thus used North Africa as a base to conquer Egypt and, in 972, shifted their capital to Cairo. The representatives they left behind in Tunisia, the Zirids, soon broke away from Egyptian rule and under the influence of Qayrawan ulama eventually abandoned Shiism as well.

The last rulers to champion any form of Shiism in North Africa, the Almohades (Arabic al-Muwahhidun, "the Unitarians"), had their initial base in another mountainous Berber region, the Atlas of southern Morocco. The regime's founder, Ibn Toumert, drew on a wide variety of Islamic teachings for his doctrines, but he did claim descent from Ali and followed the Fatimid practice of announcing himself as the infallible Mahdi (a figure sent by God to prepare the world for Judgment Day). The Almohades enjoyed remarkable success in bringing the entire Maghrib (along with southern Spain) under a single rule. But the theology that inspired their rise proved to be an obstacle in maintaining the loyalty of subjects who felt more comfortable with the established beliefs and juridical practices of Sunnism.

Ibn Toumert originally gained power in Morocco by denouncing the overly strict version of Malikism imposed on the western Maghrib by the previous Almoravid regime. However, in the long run, the Almoravids and their doctrines had a more lasting impact than the Almohades on the religious life of not only Morocco but also the Sahara and Sudan.

Up until the Almoravids' emergence in the mid-eleventh century, Islam had been represented in the desert and savannah commercial centers by small communities of Ibadi Kharijite merchants. These pioneer Muslims may have converted some Sudanic rulers and merchants to Islam, though the details of such efforts are not easy to determine. In any case, the Ibadis had only a limited concern with spreading their religion to other communities. Over time, they had become very sensitive to their vulnerable position within the Islamic world (including North Africa, where the Fatimids put an end to the Ibadi Tahert state in 909). In response to this situation, they adopted a doctrine of *kitman* (concealment of their beliefs) rather than openly confronting those who held other religious views. There is no direct evidence about whether this practice was followed in the southern Sahara and Sudan, but it would have made good sense in a region where Muslim merchants constituted a very small minority among populations with whom they wished to maintain peaceful trading relations.

By the eleventh century, the Sanhaja Berber tribes who dominated the southwestern Sahara had converted to some form of Islam. Whether Sunni or Ibadi, they were sufficiently pious to send one of their chiefs, Yahya ibn Ibrahim, on a pilgrimage to Mecca in 1036. On this journey, Yahya became aware that the Islam followed by his people did not meet the standards of orthodoxy to which he was now exposed. He asked the leading jurists in Qayrawan to find a young scholar who would accompany him back to the southern Sahara. The chosen teacher, Abdullah ibn Yasin, not only taught a very strict and militant version of Malikism to the Sanhaja but organized one faction of them into a military force with which, according to the geographer al-Bakri, "he subdued the whole desert and many of the tribes answered his call, joined his movement, and pledged themselves to follow the Sunna (orthodox Islamic path) under his direction."[5]

The resulting empire, the Almoravids (Arabic: al-Murabitun) took its name from the word *ribat*: an isolated building initially designed for military defense but later used by certain ascetic and militant Maliki scholars as outposts for spreading their faith. Ibn Yasin himself came to the Sahara not directly from Qayrawan but via a Maliki center in southern Morocco known as Dar al-Murabitin (Realm of Ribats). This is probably the basis for the use of the term by ibn Yasin and the regime he founded, although one story claims that he (following the example of Muhammad's Hijra) initially removed his followers from their tribal home to an island in the Senegal River, which served as a temporary ribat. The Almoravids first entered North Africa as allies of Dar al-Murabitin in fighting against various dissident Muslim sects (including Kharijites and Shiites) in southern Morocco. Apart from their political accomplishments, the Almoravids thus played a major role in unifying the Islamic identity of the western Sahara and Morocco.

The major energies of the Almoravids were ultimately directed toward North Africa and even Spain, but they also fought within the Sahara against the Sudanic empire of Ghana. Whether or not, as some historians claim, the Almoravids actually invaded Ghana and converted its king to Islam, the eleventh century does mark a moment when Muslim influence began to assert itself more strongly, at least among the ruling classes of the Western and Central Sudan.

Al-Bakri's description of a still "pagan" (the term used here will be "traditionalist") indigenous capital of Ghana occurs during a time when some kings in the Sudan had already converted to Islam, most notably at Takrur (in Senegambia), Gao (on the Niger Bend), and possibly a pre-imperial Mali somewhere to the south. It is not easy to judge the degree of religious commitments of men who left no written accounts of their personal thoughts and little more about their ritual practices. Stories recorded many centuries later tell of kings in Kano and Kanem who destroyed traditional shrines. Mansa Musa, among others, is said to have built numerous mosques. Yet from accounts of continuing traditionalist practices by observers, including Ibn Battuta, we know that becoming Muslim in these situations did not involve full "submission" (the literal meaning of "Islam") to the new faith but rather the extension of an existing spiritual and cultural repertoire. Sudanic sovereigns wanted to govern their own people according to local concepts of power while also dealing with the external world, which they saw as Islamic, in its terms. Even such staunch traditionalists as the eighteenth- and nineteenth-century Segu kings kept Muslim scholars at their sides to provide spiritual and practical advice as well as to negotiate with outsiders.

One well-documented, if still outward, indication of Muslim piety is pilgrimage. The kings of Mali began to undertake such voyages from the 1200s (that of Mansa Musa in 1324 is only the best known). The Saifawa rulers of Kanem possibly went on pilgrimages as early as the eleventh century and were certainly doing so by the 1200s. In 1496, the newly installed Askia Muhammad of Songhay set off on a very well-recorded journey to Mecca. While stopping in Cairo he received, like several Kanem-Borno rulers before him, formal recognition from the Abbasid caliph (a figure with no power of his own at that time) as "Commander of the Faithful" in his portion of the Sudan.

Muslim scholars recruited from within local ethnic groups begin to appear in the major commercial centers of the Sudan and southern Sahara from about the thirteenth century. These men often received support from local rulers in the form of land grants and other privileges. But, again, it is difficult to judge how much influence any clerics had on government and society at large, as opposed to the still somewhat isolated communities in which they lived. Even Askia Muhammad, who made a great effort to maintain good relations with the Islamic establishment of Timbuktu, kept his own capital down the Niger at Gao.

The same caution must be applied to the correspondence that Askia Muhammad and contemporary rulers in Agades and Hausaland carried on with well-known Egyptian and North African scholars. The most active of these advisors, the Moroccan Muhammad al-Maghili, actually crossed the Sahara in the 1490s to consult with various Sudanic sovereigns in person. His written responses to questions from Askia Muhammad indicate a more strict model of Islamic governance than was followed by most regimes in the Middle East at the time. Thus, to prevent forbidden mixing of the sexes and exposure of the body, "the Commander of the Muslims...should appoint trustworthy men to watch over this day and night, in secret and in the open."[6] Nothing even approaching this degree of enforced orthodoxy was attempted in the Sudan until several centuries later in the era of jihads.

The teachings of al-Maghili are a good example of not only strict North African Malikism but also a more general shift in the centers of Sunni Islam toward a less philosophical and more legalistic understanding of orthodoxy. The major institution of learning promoted during the eleventh century, the madrasa, emphasized the study of *fiqh* (jurisprudence), thus supporting established religion while producing graduates who could also function as state administrators. Many historians see this turning away from the classical Greek philosophical heritage and toward a narrow emphasis on law as a divergence from a path of intellectual development that would lead Christian western Europe into the Renaissance and the Enlightenment. However, within the broader Islamic world and particularly its trans-Saharan regions, medieval religious life received new energy from the formal development of mystical thought and practice under the name of Sufism.

Sufis (from *suf*, meaning wool, referring to the rough clothing of ascetics) are Muslims who claim intense knowledge of God through personal experiences of withdrawal from the secular world. Such figures appeared among the Islamic clergy from as early as the ninth century but were initially considered so controversial as to be declared heretics or even executed. By the end of the tenth century, treatises began to appear that reconciled mysticism and orthodoxy. The most influential of these works is *Ihya Ulum ad-Din* (Revitalization of religious learning), written between 1099 and 1102 by the Iranian scholar and Sufi Abu Hamid al-Ghazali. The title of al-Ghazali's book suggests that there was a problem with the existing state of Islamic thought, but he was also very emphatic in his denunciation of the already discredited Greek philosophic influences. The Almoravids condemned Sufism and even burned al-Ghazali's writings. But the Almohades included the new formulations of mysticism among the ideas that made up their own doctrine, and subsequent North African regimes often became patrons of Sufi teachers.

Sufism thus gained official acceptance as a system of thought and devotion that complemented rather than challenged established legal doctrine. Its main social influence came through practices of ascetic retreat, engagement in ecstatic religious exercises, and the veneration of great mystics of the past and their anointed successors. The ascetic aspects of North African Sufism drew directly on the tradition among Maliki scholars of moving from Qayrawan and other cities into fortified rural ribats. Among African Sufis the term for these retreats shifted to *zawiya* (settlement or lodge), suggesting their generally less militant character. However, Sufi *sheikhs* (elders or leaders) in the Maghrib and throughout West Africa continue, even today, to be known as *marabouts* (people of the ribat).

The activities carried out within zawiyas (sometimes even located in cities) included orthodox learning and worship. However, what made them distinctly Sufi were the additional exercises of *dhikr* and "saint worship." Dhikr ("remembrance") consists of repeated chanting of certain religious phrases involving the name of God ("Allah"), sometimes accompanied by *sama* (religious music and dancing). The immediate effect is to induce an altered state of consciousness that Sufis consider a means of coming closer to the Divine.

Along with the mosques and schools characteristic of all Muslim holy centers, most Sufi zawiyas in North Africa also include rounded buildings identified as the tombs of *walis* (saints; literally "friends [of God]"). Sometimes the individuals buried here are political and military figures who have taken on legendary proportions, such as Uqba ibn Nafi, the early Arab conqueror, or Idris I, founder of the first Moroccan Muslim dynasty. More often, however, they are Sufi sheikhs believed to have possessed *baraka* (literally "blessing" but more broadly "holiness" or "charisma"). This veneration of sanctified humans is understood by many historians as an accommodation between Islam and earlier, polytheistic forms of religion and has consequently received criticism from more strictly orthodox Muslims.

Sufis not only revere deceased leaders but also believe that baraka can be passed down to their descendants or close disciples. This form of Islam has thus been able to organize itself across the Muslim world into *tariqas* (literally "ways" but also "orders" or "brotherhoods") named after the founding sheikhs. To join one of these orders, a disciple has to submit to the spiritual authority of its sheikh (usually a recognized successor of the named founder) and learn his specific *wird* (prayer ritual). From the 1700s onward, Sufi tariqas based in North Africa, particularly the Qadiriyya and the Tijaniyya, played an important role in spreading and strengthening Islam in the Sahara and the regions beyond the desert.

Within the Maghrib itself, Sufi zawiyas established themselves in the countryside from at least the thirteenth century without the need for any structure connecting them to one another. Even as tariqas became more important, Muslim mystics and even major urban scholars could affiliate with them (often more than one) without any change in their activities. Most of the Muslim scholars in the trading towns of the Sahara and Sudan also studied Sufi literature and were initiated into various tariqas. Membership in these organizations had practical value in the desert, where the role of mediator among bedouin tribes depended at least as much on baraka as on learning in jurisprudence. In the 1600s Borno Sufism also helped spread Islam from cities to the agricultural countryside, which many sheikhs sought as a place of *khalwa* (retreat). However, tariqas as organizations were not especially influential in this part of the Sudan until the following century.

The transformation of Sufism from an individually adopted "way" of devotion into a more formalized brotherhood around a specific sheikh occurred in the Middle East from the fourteenth century onward and reached North Africa during the fifteenth century. These new groupings retained ties of doctrine and devotional practice throughout the Islamic world but on the regional level organized themselves as *taifas* (factions) under the direct authority of local sheikhs and their descendants. One dramatic but tragic example of Sufi entry into the central Sahara occurred on the Ahir Plateau during the early fifteenth century. The sheikh there, Mahmud al-Baghdadi, came from Istanbul and proclaimed himself a representative of the Khalwatiyya tariqa, which had then taken a strong hold among Turks. The beliefs and ecstatic rituals of this Mahmudiyya taifa caused such a shock to orthodox Muslim clerics in the Ahir capital of Agades that the ruling sultan was persuaded to send out troops and kill al-Baghdadi along with many of his followers.

The beginnings of lasting Sufi tariqa networks in the Sahara and Sudan began through the efforts of the Kunta lineage and particularly one figure, Sidi al-Mukhtar al-Kunti (1729–1811). Although claiming descent from the Arabian conqueror Uqba ibn Nafi, the Kunta were Arabized Sanhaja Berbers from the western Sahara. Like many of the elites in their community, they combined trade and religious scholarship, in this case over a wide range of centers extending from Mauritania to Tuwat in southern Morocco and the Azawad Desert just north of Timbuktu. An earlier Kunta scholar of the Western Sudan had already gained the status of sainthood, but there is no evidence that he adhered to any Sufi brotherhood, despite family traditions that make such a claim. There are reliable sources on the life of Sidi al-Mukhtar himself that tell us that he was initiated into the Qadiriyya in the central Sahara by a teacher from the Kel Intasar, a Tuareg tribe of Muslim scholars. Sidi al-Mukhtar then established a base in the original western Saharan homeland of his family. From there, he took the unprecedented step (for Saharan Africa) of proclaiming himself the regional sheikh al-Tariqa al-Qadiriyya (Chief of the Qadiriyya), in effect creating his own branch of the order.

This "Mukhtariyya" organization, eventually centered in Tim-buktu, achieved remarkable success in holding together its followers throughout a wide area of the Sahara and Sudan. A major factor here was Sidi al-Mukhtar's learning, piety, and charisma, which are recorded in numerous writings by himself and others who knew him. Sidi al-Mukhtar's own writings, citing earlier Sufi masters, stress a personalized religious devotion. The disciple "must lose himself in his sheikh so that nothing of himself is left for him." But the lengthy biography composed by Sidi al-Mukhtar's son, Muhammad al-Khalifa, stresses another key element in the order's success: a close link between piety and work in such worldly occupations as commerce, salt mining, agriculture, and animal herding. Young disciples were expected "to travel in search of knowledge" but then "concentrate on accumulating wealth.... Each one of them would become distinguished for his knowledge, piety and wealth."[7]

Sidi al-Mukhtar also benefited from the political situation around Timbuktu in the latter eighteenth century, a time when the Moroccan-based Arma regime had become virtually powerless and surrounding Tuareg tribes lacked any central leadership. The Kel Intasar, once a local military force, now functioned only as politically neutral scholars. Sidi al-Mukhtar pushed aside his former Tuareg mentors to claim both religious primacy and a major economic presence in the region. Despite some early efforts to gain support from warrior tribes for his grow-ing settlements, he soon satisfied himself with a traditional, but very expanded, position as clerical mediator.

Sidi al-Mukhtar hesitated about using his power to impose Islam on the very traditionalist Bambara Segu Empire to the south; nor did his son and successor, Muhammad, have any role in inciting the 1818 jihad of Amadu Lobbo against Segu rule in Masina. According to some oral traditions, the Kunta even allied themselves for a time with dissident Fulani chiefs in Masina in order to undermine Amadu Lobbo's rule. There is no written evidence of such subversive efforts, but surviving Kunta letters do reveal conflicts between the Timbuktu sheikhs and the Fulani theocracy of Hamdullahi over religious restrictions on economic life. More specifically, the Kunta earned a large part of their wealth from trade in tobacco, a commodity Amadu Lobbo forbade his followers to consume. Thus the Kunta leader wrote to Masina complaining of measures used to detect and punish tobacco users and cautiously concluding, "I pray that you reconsider the sanctions you have applied to this subject."[8]

During the late 1700s, Usman dan Fodio emerged as a reformist Muslim preacher in Hausaland, at the same time the Mukhtariyya was gaining strength in the western Sahara. However, instead of looking toward Timbuktu, Usman received his main outside influence from Ahir in the central Sahara through the person of a Tuareg-Fulani teacher, Jibril ibn Umar al-Aqdasi (of Agades). Jibril initiated Usman into the doctrines and practices of Sufi orders that he had himself joined in Egypt, on returning from one of his two pilgrimages to the holy cities of Arabia. These orders included the the Qadiriyya, but also those of two other tariqas, among them the Khalwatiyya, possibly with some reference to its taifa, the Mahmudiyya, which had been violently suppressed in Ahir two centuries earlier.

Usman's affinity for the Qadiriyya tariqa seems to have been more a matter of a personal spiritual choice than a dedication to any organized branch of the order then active in Africa. He wrote in later life of experiencing visions during the 1790s in which he came into direct confrontation with the Prophet Muhammad, who led him before the throne of God and then placed him under the protection of the founder of the Qadiriyya, the twelfth-century Baghdad mystic Abd-al-Qadir al-Jilani. Usman attributed his movement from preaching to jihad—something that would never have emerged from the Kunta interpretation of Sufism—directly to the actions of Abd al-Qadir:

> He sat me down and clothed me and placed a turban upon my head.
> Then he addressed me as "Imam of the Saints" and commanded me
> to do what is approved and forbade me to do what is disapproved.
> And he girded me with the Sword of Truth, to unsheathe it against
> the enemies of God.[9]

The transformation of the Hausa-Fulani jihad movement into the organizational form of a tariqa occurred only after the deaths of both Usman (in 1817) and Muhammad Bello (in 1837). The major architects of this change were Usman's posthumous son, Isa, along with his son-in-law, Gidado, who became the vizier (chief minister) of the Sokoto Caliphate. Their writings elevated Usman and Muhammad Bello to the status of saints by recounting various miracles they had performed and encouraging pilgrimages to their tombs. One motive for such new religious practices was the spread across the Sahara of another Sufi order, the Tijaniyya. The Qadiriyya and Tijaniyya competed for followers in spiritual terms, but their rivalry also had political dimensions in both the Maghrib and the Western and Central Sudan.

The Tijaniyya emerged in North Africa in the eighteenth century, an era of general Islamic reform that witnessed the rise of the al-Mukhtar Qadiriyya organization in the Sahara and Usman dan Fodio's Hausaland preaching. Its founder, Ahmad ibn Muhammad al-Tijani (1737–1815), was a Sufi marabout of southern Algeria who had a series of visions in the 1780s that instructed him to create an entirely new tariqa.

Al-Tijani presented himself as "the Seal of Wilaya [Sainthood]," meaning that there could be no Sufi orders founded after him and all the previous ones should be abandoned. In practical terms, this claim meant that he insisted on exclusive loyalty among his followers and a set of rules that rejected the "excesses" of asceticism and ecstatic dhikr associated with general Sufi practice. Given these strong assertions, the Tijaniyya initially met with a good deal of opposition. However, after its sheikh moved to the Moroccan capital, Fez, in 1789, the support of the reigning sultan, Mulay Sulayman, himself a champion of reformist Islam, allowed al-Tijani to establish an effective base for recruiting followers.

From Morocco, the Tijaniyya spread over all of northern and Sudanic Africa, although it never gained much of a following outside the continent. Its first expansion occurred in Algeria, where it played a major role in the politics of French colonial conquest during the mid-1800s. Another small branch was established in the 1790s among one of the zawiya tribes of the western Sahara, and this became the base for further propagation of the new tariqa throughout the Sudan. The most important of these new disciples was the Senegalese scholar and jihad leader Al Hajj Umar Tal.

Umar initially became a Tijani at several removes from the center of the movement. He was initiated at Futa Jallon, in present-day Guinée, by a sheikh who had joined the order in Mauritania. However, soon after this event, Umar took the unusual step for a West African so obscure and young (he was then in his early thirties) of embarking on a pilgrimage. Once at Mecca, he spent three years in the personal service of the Tijani representative there and finally received an appointment as the order's "caliph" (viceroy) for all of the Sudan. On the basis of this title, Umar later claimed the right to jihad and eventual conquest, in the 1860s, of the entire Middle Niger region, including both the Segu Empire and the Masina Caliphate.

The religious significance of Al Hajj Umar's efforts lie in their establishment of the Tijaniyya as a major force in Sudanic Islam and, more generally, the hardening of lines between competing tariqas as the basis of local religious allegiance. These sectarian politics also produced a considerable body of writing in which the Kunta Qadiriyya sheikhs and Umar himself were forced to define their positions. The Timbuktu contributions are mainly polemical critiques of the pretensions of both Umar and Ahmad ibn Muhammad al-Tijani himself to sainthood: "Whoever claims the excellence of a shaykh other than by the Prophet, I say 'By God what a lie!'" wrote the Kunta leader Ahmad al-Bakkay. "A saint is nothing more than the reflection of the moon in water."[10] Umar, on the other hand, devoted much of the lengthy period between his return from pilgrimage and the launching of jihad to composing extensive works on Sufi doctrine. His *Kitab Rimah* (Book of Spears) remains one of the fundamental texts for Tijani teaching throughout northern and western Africa.

The last of the Sufi orders to bring its own version of Islam across the Sahara was the Sanusiyya, centered entirely within the desert of the Cyrenaica region in eastern Libya. Muhammad ibn Ali al-Sanusi (1787–1859) spent his early and middle life in his native Algeria and the Islamic learning centers of Morocco and then the Arabian holy cities. His spiritual orientation was unquestionably Sufi, in an austere form that resembled the Tijaniyya. When he returned to North Africa in 1840, al-Sanusi established his own center of learning and worship in Cyrenaica, a site chosen to avoid the influence of Christian French rule, already established at this time in Algeria and threatening Morocco and Tunisia.

During the following decade, Sanusi zawiyas extended over the entire stretch of a newly established caravan route linking Waday in the southeastern Sahara with both Benghazi on the Libyan coast and southern Egypt. Like the Kunta in the western Sahara, al-Sanusi joined religious learning (he was a very serious and prolific scholar) with great respect for practical work in the material world. Oral traditions report him telling his followers, who included many manual laborers: "The paper-pushers and the praise-mongers believe they shall precede us in God's favor; but, by God, they will not!"[11] What made the Sanusiyya different from either clerical intermediaries or jihadist state-builders in trans-Saharan Africa was its assumption of virtual governance over the entire Cyrenaican interior. Sanusi settlements were well armed and included walls for defense against attacks by marauders, but they did not send military forces outward into the desert. Instead, the religious charisma of the sheikhs and an understanding of common economic interests held the system together.

If the Sanusi and jihadist theocracies constitute one extreme of the influence that Islam could wield within trans-Saharan Africa, the opposite pole is represented by Muslim scholars in the forest zones of West Africa. These ulama (or Karamoko, in the regional Mande language) emerged within the Juula merchant networks that moved southward from the western desert edge in search of gold and kola as early as the ninth-century. A second network of Hausa-speaking traders connected the forest zones to the Central Sudan beginning in the 1600s but did not develop its own system of Islamic learning.

The tradition of Islamic study and practice established among the Juula communities extending from Senegal through present-day Ghana has been given the name Suwarian. The scholars here all trace themselves back, by either biological descent or a history of study, to a legendary figure of the sixteenth century, al-Hajj Salim Suwari. Suwari himself left no writings, nor was he described in any written records of his own time, so all knowledge about him comes from oral traditions. These accounts contain a good deal of implausible information concerning Suwari's genealogy, the dates of his life, and his alleged seven pilgrimages to Mecca. Historians nevertheless accept that he actually existed and did, as the traditions assert, begin his education in the Middle Niger city of Dia (near Jenne) and then followed the gold routes south into Bambuk, near the Senegal River. Suwari brought into this Islamic frontier a distinctive set of teachings appropriate to the situation of a merchant diaspora. It combined orthodox Maliki Sunnism with doctrines of quietism (not confronting nonbelievers) and an interest in *batin* (occult Muslim learning).

Maliki learning placed a high emphasis on fiqh and insisted as well that Muslims live in regions where they had political control. This doctrine worked well throughout the Maghrib, Sahara, and Sudan, where local rulers at least professed Islam in most times and places after about 1100. In the forest zone, however, very few rulers were Muslim or accepted ulama mediation in their political affairs. Even the Islamic merchant communities there remained small and managed most of their business on an informal personal basis rather than by referring to Islamic law. Writing in these regions was largely restricted to religious uses.

Suwarians studied Maliki law, but their main guide to behavior was the sixteenth-century Egyptian scholar Jalal-al-Din al-Suyuti. During his lifetime Suyuti had advised various Sudanic rulers and visiting ulama (including, reportedly, the pilgrim Suwari) on how to follow Islam more correctly. However, in contrast to his harsh Maliki contemporary al-Maghili, Suyuti allowed some degree of tolerance for unorthodox practices. The Suwarian tradition turned this into an explicit principle in which strict Islamic observance within the community is combined with a refusal to interfere with what goes on outside it. As one of the Mande scholarly lineages, the Jabi Jahanke, states in the chronicles of their founders, "they lived independently in their own community and moved from each place where they felt their religion and community threatened. They showed respect for the local population, everyone avoiding conflict with them in matters of religious practice."[12]

Although Suwarian Islam began as an innovative blend of teachings from the available Muslim sources, it never opened itself to new ideas in Sufism, religious reform, and especially calls to jihad. In the 1800s, many of the Suwarian scholars became affiliated with the Qadiriyya Sufi order but drew from it only those elements that strengthened established positions. Thus, although the Suwarians venerated the founders of their various lineages, they did not make shrines of their tombs, nor did they perform ecstatic dhikr chanting or dancing and singing. These practices too closely resembled the rituals of surrounding non-Muslim cultures, from which the Suwarians very much wanted to keep their distance. What the Suwarians did take from Sufism was batin, the occult aspect of Islam, and this indirectly brought them closer to indigenous African religion.

Islam, like all religions, has produced a controversial belief in hidden meanings behind its literal teachings. For Muslims, this notion is applied particularly to the words of the Quran and was originally associated with Shia conspiracies against the Sunni establishment. The opposition between *zahir* (visible) and batin (concealed) religious knowledge gained broader acceptance with the rise of Sufism. It was taught by Muhammad ibn Yusuf al-Sanusi, the fifteenth-century North African theologian best known for his authoritative and highly orthodox Muslim credo.

For Suwarians, the study of batin eventually came to occupy far more of their energies than the formal learning of texts. The attractions of such occult knowledge are obvious. They gave scholars power and sources of income among not only Muslims but also much wider populations. The most common application of batin throughout the Islamic world involves the manipulation of sacred texts: sewing them into leather-covered amulets, decoding them through the assignment of secret numerical values to letters, or washing them from written surfaces into liquid potions. In West Africa, both Muslims and non-Muslims appreciated (and paid for) these practices. Some forms of batin

*This Quran from northern Nigeria contains both the words of the Prophet
Muhammad's revelations and illuminations in the only form allowed by Islam—
abstract, nonrepresentational designs. In popular religious practice, however,
both the text and the patterns accompanying them are used for magic purposes.*
Werner Forman/Art Resource

even used local plants and other substances in much the same manner as
the healers and diviners of indigenous societies.

Batin thus comes close to the syncretism (mixing Islam with other religions) that the Suwarians generally saw as a great threat in their minority
situation. However, the power of Suwarian batin depended directly on
the care its communities took to maintain outward orthodoxy and links
to the world across the Sahara. This meant that its scholars needed to be
competent in the language and content of the Arabic books that constituted their zahir curriculum and also regulate their visible public and private behavior according to the Shariah. Overt syncretism thus occurred
only on the side of the traditionalists, who incorporated elements of
Islam into their own beliefs and rituals. But such outside consumers of
Islamic learning valued what they received in direct proportion to its difference from the resources already available to them.

The world of the forest societies represents, in both economic and
religious terms, the outer limit of trans-Saharan Africa. Yet the paradox of Suwarian "orthodox syncretism," so indicative of an especially
restricted engagement with the distant Mediterranean, also exemplifies
a dialogue between Islam and local cultures that extends through all the
zones involved in cross-desert trade.

CHAPTER 5

Islamicate Culture

At the moment when Sunjata, legendary founder of the Mali Empire, confronts his archrival for control of the Western Sudan, the Mande griots evoke the force that will decide their hero's fate: "Nyama, nyama, nyama," they sing; "Nyama covers everything but nothing covers nyama." It is almost impossible and, for those who believe in it, also unwise to explain exactly what *nyama* is. But it is most certainly not something elucidated by books carried across the Sahara. Instead, like Sunjata himself, conceived from the union of a mother who transforms herself into a wild buffalo and a hunter-king father, nyama emanates from the deep bush of the savannah, far from market towns or even farming villages connected to cross-desert trade.

Yet the same griots refer to narratives like that of Sunjata as *tariku*, a term derived from the Arabic word for history. Within the story, Sunjata claims an ancestral origin among the companions of Muhammad in Mecca and prepares for his Sudanic destiny by traveling north from his forest-savannah homeland to the desert edge. There he learns more about Islam and returns homeward dressed in Muslim robes, which he also wears when proclaiming his new empire. Sunjata further speaks of himself as a successor to Dhu al-Qarnayn, the "Man with Two Horns," a name used in the Quran for the ancient Greek conqueror Alexander the Great.

The Sunjata epic provides a good example of what historians have called "Islamicate" culture. This may be a somewhat awkward term, but it helps us understand regions that are dominated, but not totally defined, by Islam. Places of this kind extend from the Middle East into Central, South, and Southeast Asia, southeastern Europe, and much of northern, western, and eastern Africa. Like other Islamicate realms, trans-Saharan Africa contains a number of different religions and ethnic groups, each with its own language, social organization, and forms of expression. All these belief systems and cultural identities had established themselves in the region well before the arrival of Arab immigrants and their Muslim faith, but it is important not to think of them as simply survivals of an earlier history. What makes even the most traditionalist of them Islamicate is their transformations, during the era of trans-Saharan trade, through a constant dialogue with Islam and its Arabic-Mediterranean culture.

Immediately prior to the Arab conquests of the eighth century, a large portion of the North African population was Christian, although many inland Berbers remained traditionalists, and a significant Jewish community had also established itself in the Maghrib. Islam very quickly obliterated all traces of North African Christianity. Adherents of this faith could still be found there, but only among pockets of foreign Europeans, whether merchant communities, military recruits, or—from the sixteenth century onward—captives from pirate raids. Traditionalism also retreated to the margins of the now thoroughly Islamic Maghrib. Some elements of earlier Berber religious practices continued in rural areas (or were at least suspected to influence Sufi rituals and beliefs). The large numbers of African slaves who were brought across the desert and concentrated in urban areas all formally converted to Islam, but they and their descendents continued to practice Sudanic rites of healing and possession that persist (and attract many "white" followers) to this day.

Among the pre-Islamic religions of North Africa, only Judaism continued to flourish. After the Christian reconquest of Iberia in the fifteenth century, both Jewish and Muslim refugees from the intolerant Spanish monarchy found a welcoming new home in North Africa. In principle, the persistence and even growth of Jewish communities during this era (in the 1800s they formed about 2 percent of the entire Maghrib population) did not compromise the Muslim character of the region. Islamic law allows Christians and Jews to practice their faith freely, so long as they accept their subordinate status as *dhimmis* (protected peoples). However, for some Muslims, in certain times and places, the Jewish population in North Africa challenged the principles of the Shariah.

"Rise up and kill the Jews," wrote the cleric Muhammad al-Maghili—the scholar who also advised Sudanic rulers on how to govern according to strict Islamic principles—in the early 1490s. "They are indeed the bitterest of enemies who reject Muhammad."[1] It is no coincidence that al-Maghili directed his Maghrib diatribes against Jewish communities in the commercial center of Tuwat at the northwestern edge of the Sahara, for Jews played a significant role in the history of desert trade. What aroused the wrath of fundamentalists like al-Maghili was the prominence Jews sometimes achieved in Maghrib economic and political life, including official designation as Moroccan Tujjar al-Sultan (Sultan's Merchants). Jewish participation in trans-Saharan trade extended along the entire desert frontier from Morocco to Libya. To some degree, participation in such a risky enterprise reflects, as in the case of Ibadi Muslims, the marginal position of Jews. But this group of Saharan merchants enjoyed special benefits from their links with wider Jewish trading networks on the North African coast, in Egypt, and across the Mediterranean into Europe. It was a fourteenth-century Spanish Jewish cartographer on the Mediterranean island of Majorca, Abraham Cresques, who produced the map of Sudanic gold routes that contains the famous image of Mansa Musa.

While the wealthiest Jews were merchants, the majority of the community practiced the more humble crafts of metallurgy and leatherwork. Muslims in both North Africa and the Sahara disdained these artisanal occupations as "impure," but they complemented the position of Jewish traders by giving them control over the processing of such trans-Saharan imports as gold, hides, and, most notably, the booming nineteenth-century trade in ostrich feathers.

Historians are not sure about the degree to which Jewish merchants actually crossed the Sahara into the Sudan. Communities of Jews certainly extended as far into the southwestern desert as Wadan and Walata. However, on the basis of the very large body of documents left by Egyptian Jews trading with North Africa during the eleventh through the thirteenth centuries, a leading scholar has concluded that they "were prevented by the injunctions of their religion to travel on Saturdays and holidays," so that as much as possible, "shipments, when going over a desert route at all, were confided to Muslim business friends."[2]

Individual Jews entered the Sudan and it is reported that Jews were expelled (along with their probably more numerous Tuwat Muslim business partners) from Timbuktu at the time of al-Maghili. But except for a brief episode in the mid-1800s, there is no evidence of a practicing Jewish congregation established south of the Sahara. More typical is the religious behavior of two Jews encountered on the Middle Niger by the British explorer Mungo Park in 1796. "They so far conform to the religion of Mahomet as to recite, in public, prayers from the Koran," Park wrote, yet "are but little respected by the Negroes."[3]

One of the conditions for Jews and others of living in a North African society dominated by Islam was the need to at least speak the local vernacular Arabic. For anyone pursuing an advanced Islamic education—whether in the Maghrib, the Sahara, or the Sudan—a thorough knowledge of classical Arabic was an absolute necessity. Thus, Arabic grammar became one of the main subjects taught within the religious curriculum. To further their mastery of the sacred tongue, students also read secular literary texts and developed an ability to write in Arabic about nonreligious subjects.

Even non-Arab Muslims who never got beyond memorizing passages from the Quran for purposes of prayer became familiar with many Arabic words. These in turn entered the vocabulary of their mother tongues and were used not only for religious matters but as terms dealing with literature (oral as well as written), commerce, politics, and even kinship. Ironically, one of the Berber groups in present-day Algeria who remain most militant in defending their language against the imposition of Arabic call themselves Kabyle—a term based on the Arabic word for "tribes."

During the centuries when Muslim merchants began to cross the Sahara, the cities of North Africa became major centers of Arabic learning. Many Maghrib authors addressed themselves to the Islamic world as a whole rather than Africa in particular. They include the great legal scholars and theologians of Kairouan, Fez, and elsewhere. Of still broader interest is Abul-Walid Ibn Rushd (1126–98), who lived in Spain and Morocco in the time of the Almohades Empire. In opposition to the general trends of Islamic thought in his era, he defended the study of Greek philosophers such as Aristotle. It is thus not surprising that his main readers at the time turned out to be Christians, and he is better known by his European name, Averroes.

One of the sciences that scholars throughout the Islamic world took up with great enthusiasm was geography. Under this heading, they wrote a great deal about the history, economy, and society of both Saharan and Sudanic peoples. But with the exception of the Moroccan Ibn Battuta (1304–68), most of these authors never traveled very far from the Mediterranean. That limitation also applies to the Tunisian-born Abd al-Rahman Ibn Khaldun (1332–1406), a thinker whose work extends well beyond the description of trans-Saharan Africa into what we would now call social science.

Ibn Khaldun is best known for his *Muqaddimah* (Introduction), in which he presents a theory of history based on the conflicts between nomadic desert communities and the more civilized populations of cities and farmlands. In his subsequent *Kitab al-Ibar* (Book of Exemplars) he attempts to apply this theory (as the rest of its title indicates) to "the Origin and History... of the Arabs, the Persians and the Berbers." This second book is less systematic, and only portions of it have been translated into European languages. Ibn Khaldun here attempts to make sense of the many divisions within Berber society by classifying their major language groups (Sanhaja and Zanata) according to his scheme of nomadism versus settlement; but the complex reality of Maghrib and Saharan culture cannot be fitted into such a neat pattern. His history is more valuable for the rich information on specific peoples and king-doms of the Sahara and Sudan that he gathered from very careful inter-views with merchants who had traveled south, pilgrims coming north, and Arab tribes living in the Maghrib hinterlands.

Literacy was not widespread within the Sudan, but around places such as the mosques of Timbuktu, scholars not only studied Arabic but also copied important books from the Mediterranean and produced many works of their own. The vast majority of these texts concern reli-gion and law, but they also include a body of secular writings, such as biographical dictionaries and historical chronicles. The biographies are mainly of other scholars, listing their pious attributes, their teachers and pupils, along with the books studied or taught with each, and their writings. If these works sound a good deal like academic resumes, it is because they were modeled on just such documents (known in Arabic as *ijaza*), which all ulama carried as their licenses to teach.

The chronicles widen this perspective only a little to include accounts of rulers along with scholars, but they remain precious as records of events in a region where no one else wrote at such length about history. The greatest of these works, *Tarikh al-Sudan* (History of the Sudan), composed in Timbuktu during the 1600s by Abd-el-Rahman al-Sadi, provides a detailed narrative of the Songhay Empire. Most of this infor-mation is presented in dry and even awkward Arabic prose that could hardly be called literary and gives no hint of the vibrant oral traditions from which much of it appears to derive. However, at moments, espe-cially when dealing with the dramatic events surrounding the Moroccan conquest of Songhay, the prose shifts into lively dialogue. It is especially interesting that al-Sadi, himself a Muslim scholar, gives the most heroic role in this story to an officer of the Songhay court known as the Hi-Koi, who represented the traditionalist fishing people of the Niger River. When the Moroccan commander invites the already defeated Songhay ruler to a meeting that turns out to be a trap, Islamic court advisors convince him to go. But the Hi-Koi wisely and courageously proclaims: "I do not trust them, but if you have definitely made up your mind, let us go one by one. If you wish, I shall go first alone. Then if I am killed the rest of you will come to no harm and I shall be your ransom."[4]

Other Arabic works of this kind draw more directly on the perfor-mance skills of Sudanic bards, whose principal job it was (and still is) to remember and recite the genealogies of local rulers and recall the heroic deeds associated with each reign. The oldest and most extensive document of this kind, the *diwan* (collection, chronicle) of the kings of Kanem-Borno, covers the reigns of sixty-seven kings from the ninth through the nineteenth centuries. It was first written down in the thirteenth century, and its prose also remains rather flat, with many accounts reduced to paragraphs such as "And next came Sultan Ibrahim, son of Sayf. His mother was Aisha daughter of Karim. His reign lasted sixteen years." But some of the biographies offer details that are more engaging and revealing, as in the story of Sultan Dunama (1086–1140), whose three pilgrimages incited such anxiety among the Egyptians that they sabotaged the boat taking him back from Mecca and "he drowned in the sea with his white garments...in the sea of the Prophet Moses."[5]

One might expect that the Arabic script would have been used to write this history in Kanuri, the common language of the very powerful and long-lasting Kanem-Borno Empire and the one in which the royal genealogies were undoubtedly first recited. Kanuri writing was used for teaching the Quran at an elementary level, but the language of more formal literacy in this portion of the Sahara and Sudan remained Arabic.

A richer example of Sudanic oral literature translated into Arabic text can be found in the "Kano Chronicle" of Northern Nigeria. This history was first written down in the late 1800s by an anonymous author with limited Islamic learning but a good knowledge of Hausa culture. Here, too, is a long list of kings, forty-eight in all, going back to the eleventh century. But in this case, the narratives of the various monarchs and their most prominent supporters are punctuated by direct citations of *kirarai* (phrases of praise poetry associated with their names). Thus one court official of the seventeenth century is evoked as "Male Elephant-lord of the town, Abdulla, like a bull hippopotamus/ Forger of chains and arrows for the foreigner."[6]

A passage such as this provides a good example of how Arabic writing could serve to record indigenous traditions that were not only irrelevant but even inimical to Islam. Referring to a ruler as an elephant not only links him to an unclean animal but also suggests that Sudanic heroes (like Sunjata and his buffalo-woman mother) drew their power from the spiritual forces of the local environment rather than a transcendent and universal God. It is not surprising that the transcription of such oral literature was never encouraged by Islamic scholars and occurred only rarely in the precolonial era.

Alongside the literary culture of the Muslim ulama, the Arabian tribesmen who invaded Mediterranean and Iranian worlds in the seventh century CE brought with them a very powerful tradition of secular oral poetry. During the early Islamic era, Muslim scholars put several collections of these poems into writing. They studied the resulting texts as a basis for understanding the words of the Quran as well as setting out an official version of the Arabic language and its literary forms. Oral poetry of this kind continued to be produced among bedouin Arabs, including the Hilali tribes who migrated into the Maghrib during the eleventh century. Such verse did not conform to the established rules of Arabic literary composition or grammar and was also difficult for outsiders to understand. Even Ibn Khaldun, one of the rare intellectuals to respect and even collect such verse, begins the text of a poem "dealing with the journey of the Hilali to the Maghrib" with the following cryptic lines: "What a good friend I have in ibn Hisham! But what men before me have lost good friends!"[7]

At some time after 1400, bedouin Arabic literature gained greater popularity among urban and settled agricultural populations and became a basis of entertainment in coffeehouses at special events such as weddings and of hospitality in wealthy homes. Performers here could not assume, as the desert bards had, that their audiences already knew the background and details of the military and amorous adventures about which they sang. They thus transformed the earlier poems into longer and more easily understood narratives known as *sira* (epics). These texts mixed poetry with prose and eventually circulated in a variety of written as well as oral versions.

The Arabic epics draw on many sources of literary and folkloric inspiration, but there is always a core reference to figures from pre-Islamic Arabia, often with some connection to Africa. These heroes include Antar, a renowned poet of that era who was born to a black mother. One of the most popular epics comes directly from the Hilali accounts of their Taghriba (westward movement) into and across North Africa. Abu-Zayd, the main protagonist of these narratives, is also black (although insistently not of African origin) and is often provoked to action by racial insults: "O black slave (*abid*), O vile one, most loathsome dog."[8]

The *Sirat Abu Zayd Al Hilali* has spread throughout the Islamic world (my Chicago dentist read it as a comic book during his childhood in southern India). Within the Maghrib, it is one of the most common themes represented in the popular art form of reverse glass painting. It has also passed from Egypt into the southeastern Sahara and Sudan, where these heroic narratives are recited among the Shuwa Arabs of Borno. It is tempting to trace the rise of oral epics in Islamicate cultures of the Western Sudan to such earlier Arabic poems. However, the Arabs in contact with this region, the Hassani of Mauritania—who are even related to the original Hilali invaders of North Africa—do not include the Bani Hilal narrative in their very rich literary repertoire.

This mass-produced twentieth-century lithograph shows Abu Zayd, the hero of the Hilali Arab forces that invaded North Africa during the eleventh century, defeating al-Haras, the leader of a local Berber tribe. Most Muslims are familiar with scenes like this one from the popular epic Sirat Abu Zayd Al Hilali, *which narrates the migration of the Hilali—a critical event in the history of trans-Saharan Africa.* Courtesy of Susan Slyomovics

The writing of non-Arabic languages in the Arabic alphabet is known throughout the Islamic world as *ajami*. This form of literacy emerged in many portions of Asia, Africa, and even southeastern Europe. The major indigenous languages of trans-Saharan Africa are no exception; all were written at some point in ajami. For the most part, such vernacular literacy, as with the Kanuri language of Kanem-Borno, served only as a support for the learning of Arabic texts. However, in some cases, especially Berber, Fulfulde (Fulani), and Hausa, a real, if still limited, literary tradition grew out of ajami writing.

Among the African languages of this region, Berber was at once the most broadly spread, the first to be written, and the least unified. In modern times, Berber is accurately described as a family of languages spoken by different peoples all of whom cannot easily understand one another. The same was probably true before North Africa became integrated into wider Mediterranean networks in the ninth century BCE. However, during the time of Phoenician and Roman colonization, the Berbers formed their own states and devised an indigenous system for writing. It is very possible that these developments could eventually have produced a standardized Berber dialect and cultural identity, but other forces dominated the region, and scholars today are unable to link these ancient North African inscriptions, labeled "Libyco-Berber," with any known language.

The advent of Islam had a mixed impact on Berber culture. During the early Muslim centuries, when different versions of Islam such as Ibadi Kharijism, Shiism, and Almoravid Maliki orthodoxy competed for the allegiance of North African and Saharan communities, the Arabic script was used to produce a great deal of religious literature in Berber languages. This practice even extended into Spain, where invading Muslim armies consisted mainly of Berbers. However, Arabic quickly became the main medium of communication for inhabitants of the coastal cities, many of whom had previously been Christian and spoke Latin. With the movement of Hilali Arabian tribes across the Maghrib and into the Sahara, from the eleventh through the fifteenth centuries, Arabic also became the language of the nomadic hinterlands, including the western Sahara. Within North Africa, Berber survived only in the protected mountain zones of Algeria (Kabylia), the larger Moroccan Atlas highlands, and some oasis communities on the desert edge. Ajami Berber writing continued in Morocco until the twentieth-century French colonial conquest, but with only limited circulation.

Berber culture remained most powerful among the Tuareg people of the central Sahara. These camel nomads also maintained a writing system, Tifinagh, based on an alphabet resembling that of pre-Islamic inscriptions. Contemporary champions of a revived Berber identity advocate "neo-Tifinagh" (a mixture of Tuareg Tifinagh and the ancient Libyco-Berber script) as a complete substitute for the Arabic and Roman alphabets. It can now be downloaded from the Internet and is being taught, as an addition to Arabic, in Moroccan schools. Among the Tuareg, however, this writing system was only employed for limited purposes, mainly by women. Aristocratic mothers taught it to their children and used it to decorate valuable objects, including the weapons and armor of their men. Outside of the home, Tifinagh was largely a graffiti medium, written on sand or stone surfaces to indicate features of the landscape to passing travelers or convey love messages.

Tuareg Muslim scholars, who viewed Tifinagh as profane and even feminized, restricted themselves more narrowly to Arabic than their counterparts south of the Sahara, who had no pre-Islamic heritage of writing. The rich secular literary production of this desert people remained oral. It includes both short poetry and stories about culture heroes whose names are sometimes derived from the figures of pre-Islamic Arabian literature. But the Tuareg never transformed these narratives into a formal genre that could be labeled epic.

Within the Sudanic zone, as in most of sub-Saharan Africa, people speak a great variety of tongues. However, from the era of the trans-Saharan trades up until the present, language use here has followed a complex pattern that links the local and global dimensions of the region. For those in closer contact with the outside world, there has been an "official" language: Arabic in the precolonial era, English or French in colonial and postcolonial times. In rural villages or pastoral encampments and in the households of urban neighborhoods, a great diversity of "mother tongues," or mutually unintelligible dialects of major languages, are maintained. A much smaller number of indigenous languages have established themselves as lingua francas for different sorts of regional business. In the precolonial Sudanic regions, four languages achieved this status: Mande, Fulfulde, Hausa, and Kanuri. Each of them, in its own way, allowed people other than Muslim scholars to participate in and contribute to the shared culture of trans-Saharan Africa.

Mande is the first of the Sudanic languages to be employed in trans-Saharan affairs. The Mande people are based in the Western Sudan, where the gold trade attracted North African camel caravans and from where local merchants traveled to the sources of this precious metal. In its present official designation, the term "Mande" refers not to a specific language but rather a family of related languages. Within this group, three of the most widely spoken tongues are mutually intelligible: Bambara (in central Mali), Malinke (in southern Mali and northern Guinée), and Dyula (in Burkina Faso and Ivory Coast). They can be considered dialects of a single language. Another more separate Mande language, Soninke, was used in the empire of Ghana and by the first merchant groups to travel from the desert edge to the gold fields. When the political reign of Mali succeeded that of Ghana, the language of the main merchant networks in this region became Malinke (called Dyula in some regions after the Mande term Juula, meaning merchant).

Mande is not only a language but also a culture with its own social practices. One of the most distinctive of these is a kind of caste system.

In Mande society, certain skilled crafts—blacksmithing, leatherwork, and the public performance of music, poetry, and storytelling—are the exclusive domain of specific lineages. These kin groups are designated *nyamakalaw* (people dealing directly with the powerful and dangerous spiritual force of nyama). The term "caste" may be somewhat misleading, as it suggests a South Asian system of hierarchy and exclusion much more elaborate than the Mande one. In this culture, it only means that individuals practicing such crafts are not allowed to intermarry with ordinary citizens and should never occupy ruling political offices. However, as in the case of slaves, nyamakalaw gathered around people in high social positions and often held more power than ordinary farmers.

This special designation of artisans is especially developed among Mande peoples but is also found in many other communities of the Sudan and Sahara, including the Tuareg, the Fulani, and the Hassani Arabs of Mauritania. Beyond this entire region and even the African continent, it is common for the occupations of metalworking, leather tanning, and public entertainment to be associated with "outsider" groups. Within Europe such roles were often linked with gypsies and Jews. Jews also dominated various artisanal professions in North Africa and the Sahara. The names and oral traditions associated with some caste groups in the Sudan also suggest Jewish connections, but it is difficult to know whether such references indicate a trans-Saharan source for these status designations or only an ideological effort—as in many other Sudanic myths of origin—to link local society more closely with Mediterranean culture.

From an Islamic perspective, all the beliefs and practices of the Sudanic "caste" systems fall in the category of "paganism." However, it was these systems that allowed Sudanic peoples to accommodate themselves so easily to an Islamic presence in their midst. Ulama (scholars/clergy) could particularly be looked on as a variant of nyamakalaw, since they, too, enjoyed technical access to invisible forces that set them apart from "normal" people. At the same time, elements of Mande culture also became identified with Islam in seemingly paradoxical ways. Thus the *komo*, a powerful and secretive local cult society presided over by nyamakalaw blacksmiths, is believed to have originated in Mecca.

It is probably because they were the first and most widely dispersed Muslim converts in West Africa that the Mande, like the Kanuri of Borno, made little use of the Arabic alphabet for literary expression. Many Mande-speakers today can write their own languages in ajami. Students in Islamic schools have long used this skill to record their translations of Arabic texts as well as instructions on such procedures as making amulets and divination. Some Mande chronicles of Muslim towns were also written in ajami; however, most of these texts amount to little more than abbreviated lists of names and offices. The more elaborate accounts of scholarly lineages focus on the great learning of their main figures; to emphasize this point (and maintain distance from the traditionalist populations among whom such ancestors often dwelt), they are almost entirely recorded in Arabic. More developed Sudanic ajami literature emerged from eighteenth- and nineteenth-century jihads, in which both Mande rulers and clergy more often served as targets than leaders.

The greatest literary achievements of Mande culture, such as the Sunjata epic, were expressed in oral rather than written form. The bards responsible for these productions in both words and music form one of the craft castes in Mande society and are generally known today as griots (a word whose origins are unclear). But as early as the 1300s, Ibn Battuta, the Arab traveler to Mali, referred to them by their Mande name as *jali* (also *jeli*) and was informed that their performance in the royal court "was already old before Islam, and they had continued with it."[9]

The musical aspect of griot performance may owe something to trans-Saharan influence. Two of the main instruments resemble ones also known from the Mediterranean: the *kora*, a harp with twenty-one or more strings, and the *koni*, a lute that is plucked like a guitar. However, the fact that historians have earlier and better records of such instruments in Egypt and North Africa does not prove that they spread from there to the Western Sudan. In any case, the kora and koni are manufactured by the griots themselves using local materials such as calabash gourds and cowhide. The koni was apparently brought across the Atlantic in the course of the European slave trade and is the possible ancestor of the American banjo.

Many griots, at least today, are pious and educated Muslims, and one subgroup of them is dedicated to performing Islamic texts. However, their main subject, like that of their counterparts among the Hausa, is the family histories of powerful men. These patrons, in turn, give money and other valuable gifts to the griots. The resulting panegyric (praise poetry) is one of the most developed forms of oral literature in all of Africa. Among the Mande, as with other peoples such as the Xhosa and Zulu peoples of South Africa, the combination of language and musical skills involved produces very rich and complex works. However, instead of telling stories about the past, these performances rely on metaphors

The kora, whose multiple strings resonate over a large gourd, is the major musical instrument of griots, the hereditary bards of the Mande culture in western Sudanic Africa. Griots' roles include praising their patrons, performing epic accounts of regional history, and acting as intermediaries in local disputes. Metropolitan Museum of Art/Art Resource and allusions; their audiences, like those of Arabian Bedouin poetry, are expected to have previous knowledge about the events that are narrated and usually, in the Mande case, to recognize the person or lineage being praised just by the melody that accompanies the words.

Ibn Battuta's observation of griot performance clearly describes panegyric. "This throne on which you are sitting was sat on by such-and-such a king and his good deeds were so-and-so; so you do good deeds that will be remembered after you."[10] Sometime after 1700, the Mande griots added a new genre to their repertoire: the epic. The disappearance at this time of the last remnants of the Mali Empire may have created a situation where the allusions in praise poetry became almost impossible to understand. One of the indigenous terms used to identify the function of epic, *maana,* comes from Arabic and is linked to the word for explaining difficult texts in Islamic religious studies. Mande griots today use it to define the epic narrative as the "explanation" of obscure praise poetry.

Mande culture thus has an indirect, yet unmistakable, link to trans-Saharan forces. The Fulani, on the other hand, more closely followed the Arabian model in developing two forms of literature: one embraced both the Arabic alphabet and Islam, and the other remained oral and tied to pre-Islamic values. The Fulani were latecomers to trans-Saharan culture, but once engaged, took a dominant role in most of the Islamic reform movements and jihads of the 1700s and 1800s. These Fulani religious efforts explain the development of Fulfulde ajami and also the later emergence of vernacular written poetry among the Hausa communities conquered by Fulani Muslim warriors. Fulfulde oral epics, on the other hand, arose independently of, and possibly in opposition to, the growth of Fulani Islamic teaching.

The Fulani are closer to the Sahara than other Sudanic peoples both in their geographical location and their racial identity. They are cattle-herders whose main base is the Sahel—the southern fringe of the Sahara. Over the course of their history the Fulani migrated from west to east across the entire Sudan. Every year, during the dry season, local herders take their herds south into the territory of farmers such as the Mande and Hausa. In one case, which became very important for literary development, Fulani settled permanently to the south in the Futa Jallon highlands of central Guinée. Physically, the Fulani are dark-skinned but remain conscious of having facial features similar to Berbers, from whom they may very well be descended. However, their language belongs to the same larger Niger-Congo family as Mande. Moreover, as rural herders without camels, the Fulani did not play any significant role in early trans-Saharan commerce or the culture connected with its urban life.

The expanded Sudanic commerce after 1500, resulting from European navigation to the West African coast, gave some Fulani new opportunities to enter market economies, settle in cities, and become seriously committed to the study and practice of Islam. In support of their efforts to teach the new faith and to win political support in their religious wars against established Mande and Hausa rulers, the Fulani began to translate Muslim texts into their own language. At first this was only done in oral form. There is evidence that a Fulfulde version of a key fifteenth-century North African Muslim text, Yusuf al-Sanusi's credo, was recited by Fulani ulama as early as the late 1600s. At that time, however, their writing of even this basic teaching was still in Arabic.

During conflicts of the late 1700s in Northern Nigeria, the Fulani leader Usman dan Fodio and his followers began to write sermons in both their own language and Hausa. Most of this literature was in verse and followed Arabic poetic models of structure and meter. Its most prevalent genre, *waazi* (Hausa: songs of warning), expresses the theology of reform, as in the following verses by Usman's brother Abdullah ibn Muhammad: "Lord God, on You we rely / For all our affairs / That You may bring us forth from the quagmire / Here in our dwelling in this world below."[11]

In order to get the specific rules of proper Muslim practice across to less learned audiences, the Fulani ulama relied on another Arabic genre, *nazm* (versified didactic prose). "Ablution before prayer, the ritual bath / Washing after emitting bodily waste, all are obligatory according to Ahmada [Muhammad]," wrote Usman's daughter, Asmau. "When it is absolutely necessary, the use of water can be omitted / This too is obligatory Sunna according to Ahmada."[12] Nana Asmau composed these verses in Hausa, which became the dominant language of the Sokoto Caliphate in the course of the nineteenth century and the main medium of its Islamic poetry up into present times. Arabic, however, remained the language of chronicles and secular writing, including political correspondence among local Fulani rulers.

Another important wave of Islamic poetic texts as well as historical narratives, always in Fulfulde, emerged somewhat later from the Fulani scholars of Futa Jallon in present-day Guinée. This region had been the site of a jihad in the 1740s, but ajami writing did not take a strong hold until about a century later, probably inspired by the Northern Nigerian example. Futa Jallon poetry also served didactic purposes, but its commandments made explicit references to Maliki legal doctrine. "Many

Fulani do not grasp what is taught to them in Arabic and remain in confusion," writes the most renowned Futa Jallon poet, Muhammadu-Samba Mombeya (1765–1851), in his *Oogirde Malal* (Mine of Eternal Bliss). "I will quote from the Fundamental Texts in the Fulani language to make them easier to understand. On hearing them, accept them."[13]

Ajami religious poetry uses the Fulani language to accomplish a goal that is more Islamic than Islamicate: turning its audience away from their own culture and toward a pure Muslim practice. But in the process of moving from a life of cattle-herding into the more settled existence in and around Sudanic urban centers, Fulani society also assimilated some features of the Mande and Hausa culture that had been the targets of jihad movements. The literary form most expressive of these secular but still Islamicate changes was the oral epic.

Long before they became engaged with the trans-Saharan economy and its culture, the Fulani had their own rich tradition of oral poetry. This literature, mainly addressing cattle and the environment in which they graze, continues today. It uses Islamic terms but in a manner that has little to do with religion. "Hey Muslims" recites one of these poets, Hammadi Hamma, using a term that could just as well be translated "Brothers."

> Send my excuses!
> As for me, since the dry season arrived I have been camped in the Great
>   Seno region
> Having no other thoughts than to water [my herd] on the trickles of
>   spring water.[14]

Herders themselves recite this poetry, without musical accompaniment. The Fulani epic, as it developed in the nineteenth century, requires the musical and verbal skills of bards using stringed instruments.

This new performance genre clearly borrows from other ethnic groups with whom the Fulani came into close contact, especially the Mande and their griots. Some of the heroes of Fulani epics are Muslim jihad leaders such as Amadu Lobbo of Masina or Al Hajj Umar Tal, but for the most part they are secular and more individualistic than historical, at least in the sense of founding states. The stories of two of the most celebrated Fulani epic heroes, Hama the Red and Sila-maka, are linked to the domination of their homeland, Masina, by the Mande Segu Empire, but they do not foreshadow the replacement of this rule by the Masina Islamic state of Amadu Lobbo. Islam enters the epics only sporadically, sometimes via such casual references as marking the times of day according to the schedule of prayers, sometimes quite perversely, as when marabouts summoned by the Segu ruler create the poison that finally kills Silamaka from the butchered and cooked remains of "a young uncircumcised albino slave...an albino mare...a totally black bull."[15]

Hama and Silamaka alternately fight and ally themselves with Segu, but by their actions they always uphold *pulakuu*, the distinctive virtues of pre-Islamic Fulani manhood. The immediate motivations for their actions are usually raiding cattle, responding to attacks on their personal honor, and making sure that their fame is properly commemorated in poetic verse. In one episode, the wife of Hama has been insulted by a Segu governor, who, she tells her husband, "says that there is no one in the Fulani country capable of avenging me. If you can, avenge me! If you cannot I will go to Silamaka...that one drinks only milk; he isn't a drinker of [Mande] millet beer like you."[16]

The tension in Fulani culture between pulakuu and Islam was recognized at the time, at least by Muslim scholars, who often denounced the epics or interpreted them as evidence of how violent and disorderly life had been before the acceptance of their religious teachings. In chronological terms, however, Islamic reform and the pulakuu assertions of epic poetry are products of the same era. Neither can be imagined without trans-Saharan trade and the economic opportunities, state-building, and cultural challenges that it produced.

Mediterranean Islam and local cultures confront one another even more dramatically in the visual arts of the Sahara and Sudan. While the architecture of this region demonstrates an adaptation of Islamic forms, especially the mosque, to African material conditions without any evident conflict, in the other arts there are serious contradictions between Islamic ideas and local "idolatry." Many less devout local Muslims and especially non-Muslims, however, refused to recognize any problems in such mixing of cultures.

Islamicate culture is most dramatically evident in the cities of the southern Sahara and Sudan. Here the general profile of square, flat-roofed masonry buildings contrasts with the round, thatched structures of surrounding villages, as well as more humble dwellings within the urban spaces. Towering over this entire landscape are the mosques, from whose minarets the presence of Islam is vocally proclaimed five times each day by the announcements of the hours of prayer. Sudanic traditions, readily taken up by foreign observers, attributed this building style entirely to the Mediterranean. More specifically, the major mosques and palaces in Timbuktu and Gao are attributed to Abu Ishaq Ibrahim al-Sahili, a poet and scholar from Granada who accompanied the Malian emperor Mansa Musa on the return from his pilgrimage to Mecca in 1325.

This frequently repeated legend is not only implausible (al-Sahili was a well-documented historical figure whose known skills did not include architecture) but also does injustice to the Sudanic crafts involved in local construction. Rectangular buildings are definitely a mark of city architecture in the Sudan, but they go back to urban developments around Jenne in the Middle Niger that preceded any direct contact with the Mediterranean. Trans-Saharan trade greatly increased the growth of cities and their associated architecture, but no general form of "palace" was imported from the north. Specific features of some of these buildings, such as rooms with cupola roofs, may have been copied from Mediterranean models, but even this form could have a local source, the arched structure of Saharan tents.

The adaptation to regional conditions is even more obvious in the mosques found south of the Sahara (and occasionally at its northern edges). As far as their religious functions are concerned, these structures meet all the demands of orthodox Islam and were dedicated not only to prayer but also the study of Muslim holy texts. Their outward appearance, however, distinguishes them from mosques in other parts of the Islamic world. The walls (especially of the highest towers) often form a pyramid, with wooden poles (*toron*) extending outward from their sides. As mosques were constructed farther south in the Sudan and into the forest, the pyramids even become cones; these structures do not create any indoor space but instead mark open-air areas for community worship.

Although the spiked mosque profile became a signature of Saharan and Sudanic urbanism, it originally evolved less as a cultural statement than as a response to the ecology of these relatively treeless zones. The basic building material is *banco* (bricks and clay dried by the sun rather than the fire of kilns). This kind of masonry can only support limited weight (thus the pyramid form) and also tends to wash away during the intensive annual rainy season (therefore the protruding poles, which are used for climbing up and renewing the clay near the end of each dry season). Fired bricks were used on a few occasions, but such items were treated as imported luxuries rather than the model for local artisans. There was simply not enough wood in the Sudan, to say nothing of the Sahara, to fuel the kilns needed to make fired bricks in large enough quantities to erect buildings. Sudanic architects and masons thus exercised their creativity and expressed their devotion through the employment of more readily available materials.

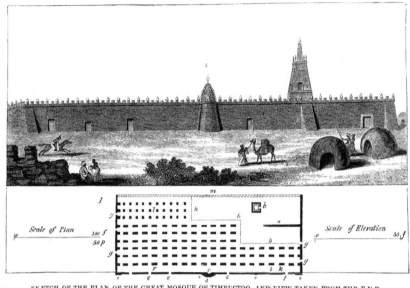

SKETCH OF THE PLAN OF THE GREAT MOSQUE OF TIMBUCTOO, AND VIEW TAKEN FROM THE E.N.E.

London : Published by Colburn and Bentley, New Burlington Street, 1830.

The Sankore mosque of Timbuktu was built in the sixteenth century and became the foremost center of Islamic learning in the sub-Saharan Africa. The towered walls shown here display the spiky, pyramidal profile of Sudanic banco (sun-dried brick) architecture and enclose a large open space used for communal Friday prayers. Manuscripts, Archives and Rare Books Division, Schomburg Center for Research in Black Culture, New York Public Library, Astor, Lenox and Tilden Foundations

One of the major uses to which wood was put in this part of Africa is the smelting of iron. Sudanic and Saharan blacksmiths produced some artistic metal goods, especially when they worked with gold or silver. Most iron, however, went into tools and weapons. The creativity of blacksmiths mainly expressed itself in another way: the use of metal blades to carve wood.

Wooden masks and statues of various kinds are the best known artistic products of both the Sudanic and forest regions of West and Central Africa. Their inspiration derives entirely from local sources. For a devout Muslim, they are doubly *haram* (unholy, forbidden). First, Islam prohibits the visual representation of the main subjects that these carvings portray: unclean animals (it is like eating them) or human beings (it usurps the creative prerogatives of God). Second, most of these carvings were produced for use in traditionalist religious rituals.

It was precisely such objects that the jihad leader al Hajj Umar Tal publicly destroyed when he captured Segu in 1852. Yet despite this opposition to Islam, African carving traditions did enter into a dialogue with trans-Saharan culture.

For the most part, the Islamicate results of such encounters reflect the culture of populations with little concern about being orthodox Muslims. However, the architects of some mosques in the region did shape their clay facades in a fashion that suggests the form of local carvings (especially the horns of wild animals) whether consciously intended or not. Muslims also employed nyamakalaw leatherworkers to decorate their own harnesses, armor, and even Quranic book covers. Sacred Islamic texts could also be placed inside leather pouches to be used as amulets. Moreover, some crafts, such as embroidering cloth, became the reserve of pious and even scholarly Muslims. The decoration of Islamic objects was not supposed to include actual pictures. Instead, the favored designs consisted of abstract shapes, often bearing letters or made up of overlapping squares. The decorative use of elaborate script (arabesque) is an entirely legitimate form of art throughout the Islamic world. The placing of such letters within squares, however, belongs to the practice of divination, performed by ulama for the benefit of both believers and unbelievers.

African unbelievers were not inhibited about going to Muslim holy men for aid in times of serious need. They also incorporated Islamic symbols into their own spiritual objects. The tunics of hunters and warriors often carried a variety of amulet pouches containing both Muslim and traditionalist power substances. Local carvers also expanded their usual depictions of ancestor figures and wild animals such as wild buffalo or bush pigs by adding to them wooden representations of Muslim scholars. Even masks representing entirely local forces might have inscriptions of Quranic verses placed inside them.

The Islamicate impact of trans-Saharan contacts did not, therefore, limit itself to the African populations who were directly involved in urban life or Muslim learning. The wide expansion of trading networks deep into the forest regions of West and Central Africa opened new horizons for both economic life and cultural expression, even when awareness of Mediterranean civilization remained very vague and remote. The advent of European colonial rule relegated trans-Saharan commerce to a very minor economic role. But the dynamic of Islamicate and even orthodox Islamic cultural change inherited from these desert contacts continued with even greater energy in the twentieth and twenty-first centuries.

CHAPTER 6

European Colonialism: Disruption and Continuity of Trans-Saharan Links

In 1823, the British explorer and naval captain Hugh Clapperton crossed the Sahara into present-day Northern Nigeria. When asked by Muhammad Bello, sultan of Sokoto, why he had undertaken such a perilous journey, Clapperton offered a probably sincere set of motives: scientific curiosity, establishing commercial routes between the Sudan and the Atlantic, and abolition of the slave trade. Muslim trans-Saharan travelers had a different view of these new European ventures. "The Arabs," Clapperton reports,

> having learned what the Sultan said with respect to the English opening a trade with his people by the way of the sea, and well knowing how fatal this scheme would prove to their traffic in the interior, probably now attempted to persuade both the sultan and the gadado [vizier] that the English would come and take the country from them.[1]

At the time of Clapperton's travels, the European presence in North and West Africa consisted only of coastal trading posts that did not threaten the sovereignty of local states, the prosperity of cross-desert caravans, or the Islamic and Islamicate culture that followed them. Yet in less than one hundred years, this entire region would come under European rule, with great consequences for all aspects of its future.

The beginning of the twentieth century clearly marks the end of trans-Saharan trade as a significant avenue of international commerce. Commodities from all of West and Central Africa now reached the outside world via rail lines, motor roads, and airplanes either moving away from the desert toward the Atlantic Ocean or passing over it without any recourse to local transport resources. New territories were carved out of the region and, even after gaining political independence in the 1950s and 1960s, took on unprecedented identities and burdens as nation-states. Islam faced challenges from both Christianity and secular modernity at the same time that Arabic and local languages had to come to terms with the official and more universal English and French.

The anxious message addressed to Muhammad Bello by the Maghrebian rivals of Captain Clapperton thus sounds prophetic. In fact, the Sokoto ruler was informed enough through trans-Saharan channels to know that by 1823 Britain had already conquered much of India and launched naval attacks against the corsairs of North Africa. Yet in order to understand the ambiguous motives and very mixed outcome of European rule in Africa, one must also take seriously Clapperton's claims of an agenda that lacked any desire for African territory and included a respect for what he called the "civilized, learned, humane, and pious" culture he had discovered on the other side of the desert.

The beginning of a serious new colonial assault on this region can be dated to April 29, 1827, only a few years after the conversations at the Sokoto court. On that day, the dey (ruler) of Algiers, angered by a quarrel over commercial debts, struck the local French consul on the arm with a fly-whisk and expelled him from an official reception. Three years later, France dispatched an army to Algeria and initiated a colonial occupation that, after many decades of warfare and negotiation, extended east and west into Tunisia and Morocco and southward deep into the Sahara.

Full foreign dominion over the territories south of the great desert sprang from what appears to be a much less trivial event. Between November 15, 1884, and February 26, 1885, diplomatic representatives of fifteen European nations plus the United States met at the Berlin Congo Conference to lay down the rules of what became known as the "Scramble for Africa." Again, much effort on the African ground (especially into the Sahara) and across European bargaining tables was necessary before colonial claims became, in the language of the times, "effective occupation"; but eventually all of North and West Africa (except for Liberia) fell under colonial jurisdiction.

It is not difficult to explain the ultimate success of these territorial conquests. Nineteenth-century Europe had undergone an industrial revolution and was able to employ larger, more efficiently organized, and, eventually, more technologically advanced military resources than could the societies of contemporary Africa or Asia. But precisely because of this wealth and power, Europeans now had far less to fear from any Africans as political rivals or to gain economically from taking over their lands than in the past. So the question Muhammad Bello asked Clapperton still remains relevant: "What are you come for?"

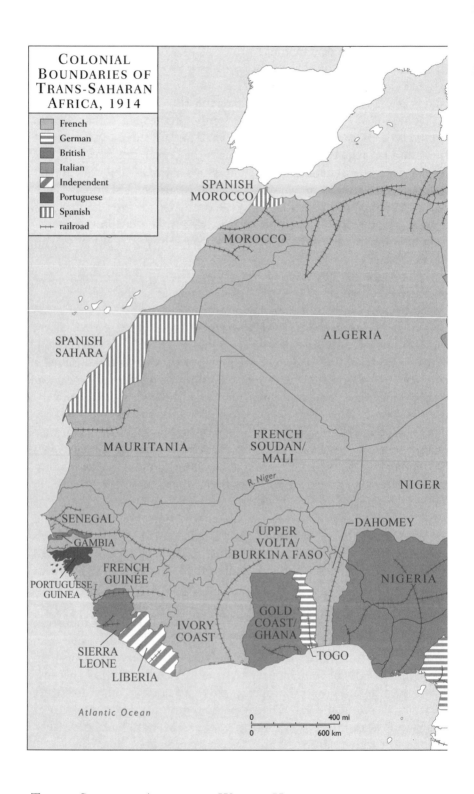

COLONIAL
BOUNDARIES OF
TRANS-SAHARAN
AFRICA, 1914

French
German
British
Italian
Independent
Portuguese
Spanish
railroad

SPANISH
MOROCCO

MOROCCO

SPANISH
SAHARA

ALGERIA

MAURITANIA

FRENCH
SOUDAN/
MALI

R. Niger

NIGER

SENEGAL

GAMBIA

UPPER
VOLTA/
BURKINA FASO

DAHOMEY

FRENCH
GUINÉE

PORTUGUESE
GUINEA

NIGERIA

IVORY
COAST

GOLD
COAST/
GHANA

SIERRA
LEONE

LIBERIA

TOGO

Atlantic Ocean

0   400 mi

0   600 km

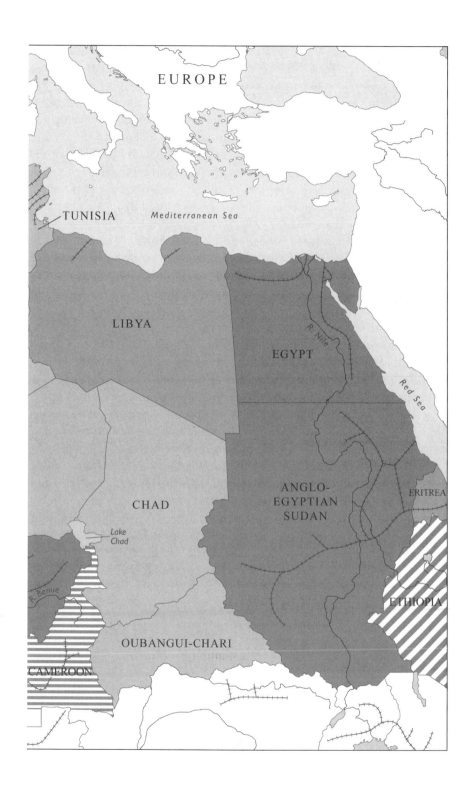

EUROPE

TUNISIA

Mediterranean Sea

LIBYA

EGYPT

R. Nile

Red Sea

CHAD

Lake
Chad

ANGLO-
EGYPTIAN
SUDAN

ERITREA

R. Benue

OUBANGUI-CHARI

ETHIOPIA

CAMEROON

Historians once expended considerable energy arguing about the deep economic causes for the dramatic European advance into the African interior. Long-standing coastal trade was clearly a precondition for nineteenth-century colonialism; colonial regimes also undertook many projects, such as building harbors and railroads, to develop the economies of their new territories; and many Europeans profited from the power their governments wielded over Africans on both sides of the Sahara. But the driving force behind the decisions to undertake such large overseas responsibilities on relatively short notice was political, based more on relations within Europe and among Europeans than any direct concern with Africa.

The original altercation between France and the Algerian dey in 1827 had to do with payment for grain shipped from North Africa to French armies in Egypt during the 1790s. France's decision in 1830 to escalate this unpleasantness into a full-scale war derived less from threats to either the nation's treasury or its honor than from the precarious position of its hereditary Bourbon dynasty, recently restored to power following the French Revolution. King Charles X hoped that a sensational military victory would revive the popularity of his regime; alas for the Bourbons, a new revolution in July 1830 removed them from the throne forever. But, as with similar American ventures in the twentieth and twenty-first centuries, it proved easier to enter Algeria than to get out, and subsequent French regimes felt bound to expand rather than contract their commitments to North Africa.

France also took a prominent role among the "Great Powers" (along with such lesser lights as Belgium) that divided up the rest of Africa after 1884. Here, again, internal anxieties about possible revolutions (social-ist this time) drove European regimes to construct nationalist economic projects that abandoned free trade for the supposed security of colonial markets and raw material supplies. But the more immediate motive was the tense international rivalry created by the emergence of a powerful new German state in the center of Europe. Effective socialist revolutions did not occur in the western European states that colonized Africa, but this outcome had little to do with the very limited economic benefits they derived from their overseas territories. The endeavor of the Berlin Conference to satisfy competing national ambitions by making every European state a winner in Africa failed much more spectacularly. In 1914, war broke out between blocs in Europe that were allied respectively (and in direct contrast to their colonial alignments) around Germany and France, and the conflict raged on for four more years, with enormous costs in individual lives, social order, and economic resources.

African campaigns during World War I were referred to as "sideshows." This designation might characterize, from a European perspective, the whole colonial venture, which came to a rather rapid end in the 1960s, less than a century after most of it had started. From an African perspective, colonialism had much more serious consequences; but the illusory and finally disillusioned nature of the European commitment to control over these lands explains why so many of the developments that emerged from the now defunct trans-Saharan trade nevertheless managed to flourish in the new era.

Among the most illusory yet persistent projects of colonialism in Africa was the construction of a trans-Saharan railway. When first proposing this transport marvel in 1879 the French engineer Adolphe Duponchel asked his readers to imagine that once the desert barrier was broken "Timbuktu merges with Algiers at the latitude of Marseille." France would thus gain access to the one hundred million inhabitants of the Sudan, a region rich in critical raw material where "we would, in exchange, dispose of the ever-increasing products of our manufacturing industries!"[2] But this particular railroad also had a political agenda, directed against both Britain—France's great colonial rival—and the desert Tuareg, who were the Africans most resistant to European rule.

Viewed strictly in terms of land mass, France was the greatest winner of the Scramble for Africa, emerging with huge tracts on both sides of the Sahara and claims to most of the terrain in between. However, Britain, which had already gained global supremacy over France in a series of world wars lasting from 1689 to 1815, also controlled richer holdings on the coasts of West Africa throughout the 1800s. At the end of the century, Britain expanded inward to take possession (as predicted in 1823) of the wealthiest and most densely populated portion of the Sudan, the Hausa and Kanuri lands of Northern Nigeria. In the continuing diplomacy that established African colonial spheres in the 1890s, the British prime minister, Lord Salisbury, found it easy to justify the apparently generous concessions made to France: "We have given the Gallic cockerel an enormous amount of sand. Let him scratch in it as he pleases."[3]

The trans-Saharan railway appeared to be one scratch that might actually offer France an advantage in African commerce. But French explorers on the ground such as Fernand Foureau saw the venture more soberly: "Considered as a business concern necessarily tying up enormous amounts of capital, I have very mediocre expectations of any return from the trans-Saharan, given the paucity of trade I have witnessed."[4] By 1904, when Fourneau made these observations, the French had also learned how formidable an opponent the Tuareg could be. They might easily have drawn such conclusions from the entire history of European travel into and across the Sahara, which began in the late 1700s. For every success—by Clapperton or the great German explorers Heinrich Barth and Gustav Nachtigal—there were other adventurers who lost their lives to bedouins. Among the most spectacular of such disasters was the death in 1880 of Colonel Paul Flatters and most of his men, the remainder of whom were forced to subsist in the desert by eating the flesh of their dead comrades. The purpose of the Flatters mission had been to scout a route for the trans-Saharan railway.

Far from succumbing to these setbacks, the idea of train traffic across the desert enjoyed several revivals all the way into the 1940s. The goal now was to create "an instrument of domination," as the economic skeptic Fourneau put it: "For this purpose alone, it will be a splendid project."[5] Up until the early 1900s the French still thought of such domination as competition with Britain for military access to the Sudan. But again, although tracks were laid from the Mediterranean into the northern Sahara, none ever came close to the projected goals of Timbuktu or Lake Chad. In 1916, when France faced the threat of a serious Tuareg rebellion in the south central Sahara, critical troop reinforcements did arrive at the desert edge by rail. However these French soldiers traveled northward from the Atlantic along a Nigerian line built by Britain, now France's ally in World War I.

Colonial rail and motorized road transport connecting the Sudan to the West African coast dealt the final blow to a trans-Saharan trade that had lost its global significance well before the late 1800s. This change did not, however, cause many immediate hardships to the populations on either side of the desert, nor was it the motivation for revolts. The only aspect of trans-Saharan commerce that European regimes interfered with directly was slave trading. However, this traffic had already slowed down considerably by the last quarter of the nineteenth century, due to prohibitions imposed (under pressures from Europeans) by the Ottoman and Egyptian governments.

Other forms of commerce accommodated themselves to European rule and even profited from the new political situation. The Maghrib now ceased to be a major economic partner of the Sudan, but this relationship had always been of more importance to societies at the southern end of the Sahara than to those in the north. Sudanic merchants and producers only abandoned trans-Saharan trade because they had better commercial opportunities to their south. In fact, railroads were so much more efficient than camel caravans that the Sudan could now export not only traditional commodities, including cattle hides and goatskins, but also a whole new range of goods such as peanuts and raw cotton. African, specifically Mande, appreciation for the economic advantages of colonial rule is expressed by the late-twentieth-century Ivoirian novelist Ahmadou Kourouma: "What matters most to a Malinke is freedom of trade. And the French, also and above all, stood for free trade that allowed the juula, the big Malinke traders to prosper."[6]

Even Saharan caravan leaders and Sudanic manufacturers of goods such as textiles and leatherwork profited from the colonial expansion of regional markets. European administrations, in order to maintain their presence in the desert, required the services of Saharan camels and their Berber or Arab owners. If very few commodities now traveled the entire length of the Sahara, goods produced within the desert or at its southern edge, such as handicrafts, salt, and dates, along with livestock herds and their many by-products (and even some slaves), still found buyers in the desert and among the growing populations in the Sudanic agricultural zones.

The major economic problem in the regions bordering the desert remained drought, and here colonial rule, even when well intentioned, made things a good deal worse. The years 1903–14 witnessed a major drop in rainfall throughout the West and Central Sudan, leading to extensive famine. A French administrator, Eugene Lenfant, described the landscape around Lake Chad during this era: "Poverty on every side. Poverty of broken land baked by the sun; poverty of the burning dunes of Borno...nothing but poverty from Kanem to Waday."[7] Continuing colonial military campaigns and tax demands during this period exacerbated these problems and offer one explanation for the many local revolts against European rule. But French efforts to remedy the drought and resulting famine accomplished little and sometimes increased local hardship. In 1928, Jean Tilho, a colonial official and explorer, proposed building a dam on part of Lake Chad that would provide not only irrigation but also hydroelectric power for the neighboring Cameroon railway! Fortunately, this entirely unrealistic project (apart from costs, the lake was already shrinking), like the trans-Saharan railway, was never put in place.

However, in justifying his plans, Tilho mentions another measure that the French undertook throughout the cattle-grazing zones of the West and Central African Sahel: boring new and deeper watering wells. The resulting growth in animal herds eventually produced overgrazing, thus increasing pressure on other resources of the area, especially soil and grass. As a result, during the next extended cycle of low rainfall (beginning in the late 1960s, after the end of colonial rule), the Sahel experienced a major ecological catastrophe from which it has not yet fully recovered.

The colonial powers did not gain much wealth from rule over trans-Saharan Africa. Individual European groups and firms profited from their privileged positions in Africa, but this did not usually bring great benefits to people back home. Algeria provided the starkest example of such problematic private colonization, since its best lands fell into the hands of white settlers. About half of these privileged immigrants were not actually of French origin, and the crops they produced (wheat and wine) competed with France's own agriculture. The home government also granted Algerian settlers the rights and political power of French citizens, which meant that the subjugated Arab-Berber majority population were only able to win independence through a long and very bloody war.

Elsewhere in the Maghrib, and especially the Sudan, settlers were sparse and investments by European businesses remained limited. While taxation often placed great burdens on the colonized peoples, its purpose was mainly to cover the costs of administration rather than to enrich the home country. The French, whose sub-Saharan possessions were organized into West and Central African federations, did sometimes use revenue surpluses from richer territories to cover deficits in the poorer ones. But this only shows how marginal the colonies were to European economies.

After a railroad across the desert was recognized as unprofitable, none of the colonial development projects that followed can be seen as "trans-Saharan." Instead, undervaluation of trans-Saharan communications now justified European schemes for radical economic transformation of the Sudan. In comparing the development of the Nile Valley to that of "our Nigerien Sudan," yet another French engineer, Ernest Belime, argued in 1925: "While from Alexandria, to Babylon, from Athens to Rome, human knowledge increased through the successive contributions of all the Mediterranean people, the black races, separated by vast desert spaces from the civilized world, lived in stagnant barbarism."[8] Belime's "civilized" solution to Sudanic ignorance, a project for massive irrigation of Mali's inner Niger Delta, received considerable criticism from other colonial technocrats. However, unlike the phantom Saharan train tracks, the Office du Niger actually took shape on the ground, absorbing huge amounts of overseas investment and local, often involuntary, labor from the 1920s through the first decades after Mali's independence. The idea had been to cultivate large quantities of cotton for export and rice for local consumption, but the results proved very modest at best.

Given their generally limited economic interest in African colonies, colonial regimes attempted to govern these territories at a minimal cost. One means of cutting expenses was to support rulers already in place. Thus when France extended its Maghrib empire beyond Algeria, it did not attempt to clear new space for troublesome European settlers but classified Tunisia and Morocco as "protectorates" with the hereditary monarchs still reigning. In Morocco, where French rule lasted for fewer than fifty years, the monarchy survives to this day as the main center of national power.

Within the Sahara and to its south, no single precolonial state could claim authority over any of the newly created European territories. Moreover, the jihads and other wars of the nineteenth century had left much of the Sudan, especially the western region claimed by France, in a state of turmoil at the time of European conquest. Farther east, in Northern Nigeria, the Sokoto Caliphate remained intact, although its ruler fled the country rather than accept colonial domination. Immediately after occupying Sokoto in 1903, the British high commissioner, Sir Frederick Lugard, simultaneously convinced the local councilors to appoint a new sultan and announced that the successors of Usman dan Fodio "have by defeat lost their rule, which has come into the hands of the British." Lugard and his followers later developed his combination of European territorial sovereignty and local political continuity into a formal doctrine known as indirect rule, which was applied throughout British tropical Africa and defined in Lugard's canonical *Political Memorandum* (1918) as "rule through Native Chiefs, who are regarded as an integral part of the machinery of Government."[9]

Nonetheless, final authority over local districts remained, even in the British colonies, with European administrators who had the right to intervene in all aspects of local government. But a very small number of administrators took responsibility for vast regions and populations about whom they often knew little. Thus, their theoretically despotic power could only be exercised with the aid of paid African subordinates. As described in the memoirs of Amadou Hampâté Bâ, a former West African colonial clerk, when the French "commandant" had to undertake a serious action,

> He immediately called together his personal general staff, consisting
> of the interpreter, who was at once his mouth, his eyes and his ears;
> the chief clerk, who was the keeper of his seals and the writing
> instrument of his sultanic decrees; and the police sergeant, who was
> his archangel, head of the guardian angels of Hell, which is to say the
> prisons.[10]

For Islamized populations near the Sahara, including the Sokoto rulers, this aspect of the new political order struck a special blow against their status, as most of the clerks came from regions closer to the Atlantic, where the European education required for such employment spread more quickly. Hampâté Bâ, as indicated by his first name (Amadou: Ahmad), was a Muslim—recruited, against his very pious family's will, from a Quranic school into a French one. But Hampâté Bâ's story runs against the grain of the general respect that both French and British colonial regimes showed for Islam, a policy that maintained and even enhanced the cultural legacy of trans-Saharan trade.

In light of twenty-first-century hostilities between radical Islam and the European-American "empire," collaboration between colonial regimes and Muslims may appear surprising. Indeed, Islamic regimes and Sufi brotherhoods very vigorously opposed the Europeans while they were still establishing control over their African territories. Moreover, both French and British colonialists allied themselves to antislavery movements, which, by the late 1800s, were led by Christian missionaries who were hostile to Islam on both religious and humanitarian grounds.

Despite these initial antagonisms, under colonial rule Islam maintained its dominance in the Maghrib and the Sahara while expanding more widely and deeply throughout Sudanic West and Central Africa. Even in the forest regions, where Christianity did have a major impact at this time, the spread of Islam also continued. This apparent paradox can be explained by three factors. First, the long history of Islamization in this region could not be reversed in a relatively brief period of European governance. Second, the economic and social changes that colonialism introduced or accelerated were precisely those that had encouraged conversion to Islam in earlier times: expanded commerce, urbanization, and the spread of literacy. Finally, the conservative and underfinanced colonial regimes recognized Islamic leaders, usually the heads of Sufi brotherhoods rather than precolonial states, as "native rulers" who could serve them as political intermediaries.

In the first stages of colonial conquest, Islam played a major role in resistance against European rule. Almost immediately after France's 1830 seizure of the city of Algiers, the sheikh of the local Qadiriyya order, Abd al-Qadir, organized the previously anarchic hinterland of Algeria into a formidable political and military force. Well informed about not only Islam but also modern military technology and the domestic politics of a French nation somewhat dubious about enlarging the costs of North African occupation, Abd al-Qadir made a number of diplomatic efforts at dividing Algeria between his own realm and the new French

Abd al-Qadir al-Jazairi led Algerian resistance against French colonization during the 1830s and 1840s. He combined skills in warfare and diplomacy with the authority of a Muslim scholar. A combination of superior European military resources and rivalry among local Sufi brotherhoods finally led to his defeat.
Library of Congress LC-USZ62–104871

coastal colony. But in appealing for support among the diffuse Algierian communities, he resorted to the language of jihad. "It is my duty to rally you to my banner," he wrote in 1833 to a Turkish leader. "Let us therefore efface all the racial differences among true Muslims.... and let us all have one armed hand raised against the enemy."[11]

Abd al-Qadir finally surrendered to the French in 1847, mainly because of European military superiority, and went into exile.

The European colonizers also used dissension among Algerian Muslims to win the voluntary support of a rival Sufi order, the Tijaniyya. The Tijani headquarters at the Ain Mahdi oasis in southern Algeria figured in Abd al-Qadir's plans for a last line of Saharan defense against the European invaders. But because of both religious competition and memories of earlier divisions in fighting the Turks, the Tijanis refused to cooperate with Abd al-Qadir, who destroyed Ain Mahdi in 1838. One year later, Muhammad al-Saghir al-Tijani, son and successor of the order's founder, offered his political support to the French, denouncing Abd al-Qadir, "who does not know the rules which exist among the powerful, for he is a bedouin, and the bedouins do not understand any of this, as it is written in the books of the learned."[12]

On the basis of alliances with such compliant elements of the Muslim establishment, the French eventually governed the indigenous population of Algeria on terms similar to those of their Ottoman predecessors. The new European authorities claimed ownership of *habus* (land and other property set aside for the support of mosques and Quranic schools). From these and other public funds, they paid, appointed, and supervised the ulama, who provided the various judicial, educational, and ritual functions of an Islamic society.

Further south in the Sahara and Sudan, the status of Islam and its relationship to a broader African society was not as clear. The French again found themselves fighting against Sufi leaders before turning some of them into allies. Much of this antagonism derived less from Islamic hostility to Europeans than French panic, as illustrated by the case of the Sanusiyya in the desert east of Lake Chad. The founder of this order, Muhammad ibn Ali al-Sanusi, was an Algerian who had refused, in the 1840s, to live under French rule. But he chose, like the defeated Sokoto caliph in 1903, to leave the colonized territory for Mecca rather than prolong armed combat. The best informed French observers recognized the commercial rather than political purposes of the Sanusi zawiyas (lodges) that extended deep into the Sahara through Cyrenaica in eastern Libya. But in the context of late-nineteenth-century colonial competition, a different image of the Sanusiyya reached the European public, first from the 1884 writings of a Saharan explorer and scholar who should have known better, Henri Duveyrier, and then from Jules Verne, author of *Around the World in Eighty Days*. Verne's 1885 novel *Mathias Sandorf* repeats Duveyrier's account of the Sanusiyya as a vast conspiracy, stretching across all of Africa and "a permanent danger to the European establishments in North Africa."[13]

This legend of the Sanusiyya turned into a reality when it became a basis for attacks on them from both the south and north. In 1902, a French commander in the new colony of Chad, Georges-Mathieu Destenave, became convinced that the Sanusis were nothing more than anticolonial slave traders who had built across the Sahara "an immense scaffolding of lies, hypocrisy, hate and the exploitation of human credulity that they have covered over with a veil of religion."[14] The Sanusis fought off the ensuing French military campaign for another decade, and even after their defeat they played a major role in the Tuareg uprising against colonial rule during World War I. Beginning in 1911, Libya also came under assault by the Italians, who quickly took over most of its territory from its prior Ottoman rulers. But in the Cyrenaica region Sanusi resistance continued until 1931, led first by the successors of Muhammad ibn Ali and then by Umar al-Mukhtar, a guerilla fighter and scholar who in defeat became a modern Libyan national hero, just as Abd al-Qadir did for Algeria.

South of the Sahara, even in the Sudan, Islam had not achieved, by the end of the nineteenth century, the same degree of hegemony as in the Maghrib or even the desert. Its greatest penetration was probably in Northern Nigeria, and there, as early as 1903, Lugard could promise the vanquished Sokoto rulers that the colonial "government will in no way interfere with the Mohammedan religion."[15] As a guarantee of this pledge, the British limited the access of Christian missionaries—elsewhere a major pillar of their colonial ventures—to this region. France also restricted missionary activity in its portions of Sudanic West and Central Africa, but less out of respect for Islam than due to the hostility, from the early 1900s onward, between the secularist French Third Republic and the Catholic Church. (Protestant missionaries also came under suspicion as foreigners.)

The same anticlerical attitudes sustained a debate among French administrators about how to deal with marabouts, the Sufi leaders found throughout the region. Although conspiracy theories like those about the Sanusis continued to exercise some attraction, by World War I the colonial experts of the "service des affaires musulmanes" came to a consensus about a distinctive *Islam noir* (black Islam) that was adapted to various local African cultures and thus did not seriously threaten French interests. "The black mentality" wrote the foremost of these scholar-administrators, Paul Marty, "is completely incapable of bearing the metaphysical concepts of the Oriental Semites and the ecstatic digressions of the Sufis."[16]

The 1913 study in which Marty made this statement addressed a specific Sufi order, the Murids (a Senegalese offshoot of the Qadariyya) whose leader, Ahmadu Bamba Mbacke, had been exiled by the French but eventually allowed back among his followers. Despite the condescending and racist tone of Marty's analysis, it does support a colonial policy allowing Sufi leaders to acquire not only spiritual authority but also material wealth. In the case of Ahmadu Bamba, who used his pupils to grow peanuts for export, the European regime recognized a common interest in producing cash revenues. "Although it is possibly regrettable that we have allowed this Mouride power to establish itself," stated a French political report of 1926, "from an economic viewpoint the action of the Mourides has contributed enormously to the development of agricultural production in the region of Baol."[17]

The other major Sufi order extending across the Sahara, the Tijaniyya, initially played a very different role in the colonial politics of the Sudan than it had in Algeria. Al Hajj Umar Tal, the great Tijani jihadist leader, clashed with the French in the Senegal Valley before founding his own empire in the Middle Niger during the 1850s. Three decades later, Umar's sons and successors led the resistance against French expansion toward the desert edge. However, once the French firmly established their military supremacy, they recognized that the religious prestige of Umar could be turned to their advantage, and in the early 1920s they unofficially but very publicly appointed one of his grandsons, Seydu Nuru Tal, to the position of "Grand Marabout" for all their West and Central African colonies. Here, too, both sides profited, as the Tijaniyya expanded its prestige and membership and the colonial authorities could count on exhortations to loyalty such as the following, delivered by Nuru Tal in 1940 during the first year of World War II: "France, the protector of Islam, is in danger. Our happiness, the free exercise of our faith, our very existence are all insolubly tied to the fate of France. When a house catches fire all its occupants hasten to put out the flames."[18]

However tolerant and even supportive colonial authorities may have been toward Islam as a religion, they also represented a secular Western culture that threatened to displace the Islamic Mediterranean as the reference point for Africans seeking their place in a wider world.

The vehicle—some would say "gift"—the European regimes offered for bringing this culture to their new subjects was the school. But colonial schools in this region faced two dilemmas: first, how much to invest in educating populations who had no political means to demand such benefits and who might best serve the limited ambitions of their rulers if most of them remained within their own cultures, and second, what to do with the systems of schooling and literacy inherited from prior centuries of exposure to Islam.

Algeria, the first territory of this region to be colonized, presented a special challenge to its French rulers, who had to deal here not only with Muslim African subjects but also European settlers who used their political influence to "keep the natives in their place." The solution finally arrived at by the very secular and nationalist Third Republic was to maintain and supervise Quranic schools while offering a small number of Algerians the opportunity to become very modest versions of Frenchmen. "The goal of the education given to natives," stated the key plan for secular schooling of 1898, "is to make them into decent, enlightened, prudent, hardworking men, drawn to us by the use of our language and recognition of the progress in which we allow them to participate with the aim of improving their well-being, their hygiene, their agricultural practices and their industrial labor."[19]

In Tunisia and most of Morocco, the French left education mainly in the hands of local authorities, who maintained Arabic as their principal medium of instruction though also recognizing the need to teach French. At the other extreme, in France's sub-Saharan Africa territories, government-sponsored education was entirely in French.

Schools in British colonies operated on very different principles, partly because of conditions in the regions occupied but also due to the ideas and practices imported into Africa. Both at home and in its colonial empire, Britain relied on religious bodies to provide a large proportion of educational services. In Africa this meant missionaries, whose contributions of labor and funds not only extended considerably the amount of schooling that could be offered but also placed an emphasis on local languages, already studied and used in efforts to make Christian converts. Unlike the French, who since the early 1800s felt compelled to defend their language against "les Anglo-Saxons" (the British and Americans), the British feared a repetition in Africa of their Indian experience, in which the graduates of local English-language schools felt empowered to make unwelcome claims for self-rule by the end of the century. Typically, British colonial schools in Africa used and taught local languages exclusively in the primary grades, introduced English as a subject somewhat later, and made it the medium of instruction only for relatively advanced education.

In Northern Nigeria, the British therefore supported not only the Sokoto Caliphate and Islam but also the literary development of the Hausa language. Hausa had already in the early nineteenth century become a written language, using the Arabic alphabet, but these efforts were dedicated almost entirely to religious poetry. Immediately after conquering the region, British administrators concluded that in order for Hausa to serve their own administrative needs, it had to be written in the Roman alphabet. For decades, however, local scholars and rulers resisted such a change because they connected it with not only the abandonment of Islam but also the proselytizing efforts of Christian missionaries (who did operate at the fringes of Hausaland). Finally, in the 1930s, government educational authorities established a Literature Bureau and persuaded a group of young Quranic scholars who had been trained as schoolteachers to write short historical novels in romanized Hausa—"a conception," as Rupert East, the responsible British official, reported, "which was entirely new, and of doubtful value, if not morality."[20]

Despite such a forced beginning, secularized and romanized Hausa literature did take off to become a vibrant modern vernacular medium. One of the novels of the 1930s, Shaihu Umar, is still read today and tells the very trans-Saharan story of a Hausa boy kidnapped into slavery, educated at the northern desert edge, and finally returned home as a Quranic teacher. The author, Alhaji Abubakar Tafawa Balewa, later became the first prime minister of postcolonial Nigeria. But his assassination in 1966—the prelude to a bloody civil war—indicates the problems that could arise from a split between the Saharan and Atlantic orientations of modern West Africa. Such a division may have served short-term British interests by slowing down—but not stopping—the drive to independence initiated by southern Nigerians, more fully initiated into European culture than their northern compatriots. But it also left a legacy of religious and regional conflicts that continue, often in violent form, to this day.

In the French colonial zones of trans-Saharan Africa, traditions of ajami vernacular writing had to struggle on their own. France also practiced policies of "divide and rule" in its portions of trans-Saharan Africa, but education in local languages played almost no role here. In the Berber-speaking regions of southern Morocco, the French set up what they called Ècoles Franco-Berberes (Franco-Berber schools), but all this meant linguistically was the exclusion of Arabic (and in this case

Islam) in favor of French and secularism. "Arabic is a factor of Islamization, since it is the language of the Quran and our interest directs us to bring about an evolution of the Berbers outside the framework of Islam," wrote Marechal Hubert Lyautey, the "French Lugard," in 1925. "From the linguistic point of view we must set a direct passage from Berber to French."[21]

The politics behind these cultural efforts became more apparent in 1930, when French authorities pressured the Moroccan king to issue a dahir (decree) declaring that "in the interest of the welfare of our subjects and the tranquility of the state" it was advisable "to respect the customary legal status of the pacified Berber tribes."[22] The Moroccan elite easily recognized this "Berber Dahir" as an assault on Islam and thus, contrary to French intention and the Nigerian example, used it as a basis for unified nationalist opposition to the European regime.

None of the Sudanic languages that had developed ajami writing systems in the precolonial era received sustained support from the

Marechal Hubert Lyautey conquered Morocco for France in 1907–12 and then served as its resident general (effectively governor) until 1925. His military and administrative successes were marred by an effort to divide Berbers and Arabs, a policy that Moroccans experienced as an attack on Islam and a spur to anticolonial nationalism. Library of Congress LC-DIG-ggbain-26038

French educational establishment. Nonetheless, such literacy continued and even expanded through the efforts of unofficial promoters, including ulama, secular African intellectuals, and European administrators acting as private scholars. Wolof, the main language of Senegal, had never been widely written in the precolonial era, but the dynamism of the Murid and Tijani Sufi brotherhoods produced an extensive new religious literature using both Arabic and Roman scripts.

Futa Jallon, in what became French Guinée, remained a major center of Fulfulde religious writing in ajami, but the poets of the early 1900s moralized about a colonial situation in which

> Allah has put us to a test; that is why he has made us live in the time of [French] tax collectors, those men who are cut off from the Joy of the Afterlife.
>
> *   *   *
>
> Give Them their tax, so that they may eat it and we others can follow our religion; Allah will repay us with nourishment in the Afterlife
> But those who eat the taxes with them, let them know for sure that they will go with them into the fires of Hell in the Afterlife.[23]

Despite its rich history, Fulfulde writing could not challenge the hegemony of either Arabic or French, because its cattle-herding speakers remained scattered as minorities across a wide range of West and even Central Africa. By contrast Mande, in its various but mutually intelligible forms, remained the most widely spoken of the Western Sudanic languages. If Britain had ruled this region, it is very likely that a standardized Mande would have become a vehicle of both early education and literary production. Under French rule a northern Guinée intellectual, Suleiman Kante, took it upon himself in 1949 to invent a new phonetic alphabet, N'Ko (meaning "I speak"), for the core Mande languages of Malinke, Bambara, and Dyula.

The impetus for Kante's effort came, according to those who remembered him in 1993, not from Europe but from the Arab-speaking world, more specifically a 1944 Lebanese book denigrating Africans because their languages were supposedly not written. N'ko, like Fulfulde poetry, posed no threat to the French; but their comforting conception of Islam noir, as well as the Islamicate culture that lent it some validity, did find itself challenged, in the last colonial decades, by Arabic as both the vehicle and emblem of new religious forces from the Middle East.

These teachings no longer needed desert caravans to spread within Africa. Under colonial rule, African Muslims could make pilgrimages to Mecca or travel to Mediterranean centers of Islamic learning far more easily than in the past, using motorized vehicles across the Sahara, Atlantic shipping, or—as the twentieth century progressed—airplanes. Moreover, the new forms of Islam combined a fundamentalist desire to return to religious roots with a modernist effort at incorporating Western scientific thought and technology into religious orthodoxy. The early proponents of this new religiosity did not attack colonialism directly but rather its patronage of "corrupt" Islam, particularly Sufi brotherhoods.

Reformist Islam emerged in the Maghrib a good generation before it became active in Sudanic Africa. In 1931, a group of scholars trained in the Middle East, led by Abdelhamid Ben Badis, formed the Association of Muslim Algerian Ulama (AUMA), with—its vice-president declared two years later—"two noble aims: to restore the dignity of the Islamic religion and to restore the dignity of the Arabic language."[24] In 1936, Ben Badis and his associates denounced Sufi practices as "worthy only of the age of paganism" and their promotion by colonial authorities as aimed at "showing us to be backward and superstitious."[25] The AUMA did not directly challenge French rule, which Ben Badis considered necessary for Algeria "to make progress on the road towards civilization and development." But in 1936, the AUMA leaders declared themselves to be members of an "Algerian Muslim nation [that] is not France....It does not want to become France." At the same time, they evoked French principles of separation of church and state to demand that they, and not the colonial regime, should control Islamic charities, mosques, and schools.[26]

In 1952, Marcel Cardaire, a colonial "pilgrimage officer" (charged with supervising the hajj), reported that he had found five hundred students from French West Africa studying at the Islamic university of Al-Azhar in Cairo. Moreover, they told him that "the traditional leaders of Islam Noir" were "ignorant and greedy" and on returning home, "we will need to wipe out these bad pagan and westernized Muslims."[27] In an attempt to counter the Arabic-media teachings of Muslim reformers, Cardaire organized one of the rare French efforts to promote literacy in West African languages, but without much success.

By this time, in any case, colonial rule throughout trans-Saharan Africa was coming to an end. In both the violent struggle for Algerian independence and the more peaceful transitions in tropical French and British Africa, individuals educated in European languages and culture rather than Islam led the nationalist movements. Yet this triumph of westernization was a good deal less than complete. The early African postcolonial regimes proved unable to meet their promises of economic and social development. One of the outcomes of the resulting disillusionment has been a renewed growth of Islam and further conflicts among Muslims in both the Maghrib and Sudan over competing forms of their religion and its role in regulating social life.

During the late twentieth and early twenty-first centuries, the Sahara has still provided some links between Africa and global concerns, though very differently than in the glory days of camel caravans. The major economic asset of the desert is now the large, high-quality petroleum reserves lying beneath its northern soils. Land and air traffic traverse the Sahara carrying some of the wealthiest people in the world ("adventure" tourists) and some of the most impoverished (clandestine migrants from tropical Africa hoping to reach Europe via the Maghrib). In 2003, the European Command of the U.S. military announced a $100 million "Trans-Sahara Counter-terrorism Initiative" based on beliefs (questioned by scholars) that organizations associated with al-Qaida were using the desert as a strategic base. Added to this mix are continuing disputes over the former Spanish territory of Western Sahara ("Africa's last colony"), periodic Tuareg revolts against Sahelian governments, and genocidal attacks of Arabic-speaking pastoralists from the Nile Valley on the populations of Darfur.

The Sahara has thus again become what it was in Carthaginian and Roman times—a contested and perhaps dangerous zone beyond the edge of the familiar world (or, now, of two such worlds, a Mediterranean and a Sudanic one) rather than the thriving highway of its own African world. The history of that highway still tells us a good deal not only about how our entire globe became integrated in the past but also how Africans on both sides of the desert and within it continue to shape their identities.

Chronology

3000 BCE–300 CE
Physical formation of the present-day Sahara from previous Holocene (wet) phase

814–146 BCE
Colonization of the North African coast by Carthaginians, Greeks, Romans

ca. 450 BCE
Desert trade route described by Herodotus

ca. 400 BCE–300 CE
Garamantes flourish in Fazzan region

ca. 100 BCE/CE
Camels reintroduced into Sahara

642 CE
Islamic (Arab) invasion of North Africa

800 CE
Beginnings of trans-Saharan trade by Ibadi Muslim sect

900s–1500s
Sudanic empires flourish

1000s
Almoravids impose Sunnism, Maliki law on western Sahara, Maghrib, and Sudan

1200s–1400s
Drought in Mauritania, southwest Mali; Western Sudan trade shifts to Niger Bend; major gold sources now Bure and Volta River basin

ca. 1250
Sunjata founds Mali Empire

1332–1406
Life span of Abd al-Rahman Ibn Khaldun, historian and social anthropologist of Maghrib, Sahara, and Sudan

1400s
Europeans arrive on West African coast

1493–1538
Askia Muhammad rules Songhay

1500s
Spain, Ottoman Empire, and Morocco struggle over North Africa

1500s
Rise of Hausa cities (Northern Nigeria) as trading centers

1571–1603
Idris Alauma rules Borno

1591
Moroccan Sultan Ahmad al-Mansur conquers Timbuktu

1656
Abd-el-Rahman al-Sadi completes *Tarikh al-Sudan*

1600s to 1800s:
Jihadist movements and regimes in the Sudan

1804
Usman dan Fodio founds Sokoto Caliphate

1818
Amadu Lobbo founds Hamdullahi in Masina

1830
French invasion of Algeria begins modern colonial era

1852
Al Hajj Umar Tal begins conquest of Middle Niger region

1884–85
Berlin Congo Conference sets ground rules of European "Scramble for Africa"

1900s
Colonial railroads replace Saharan caravans in international trade with Sudanic Africa

1952–1962
Maghrib and West Africa regain independence

Notes

CHAPTER 1

1. Sudan, the modern country of diverse geography south of Egypt, is not a central focus of this book. Where it does come up, it will be referred to as the Nilotic Sudan. When "Sudan" is used without qualifiers, it refers to the regions also known as the Western and Central Sudan, all located between the Sahara and the forest zones of West and Central Africa.
2. Hanno the Carthaginian, *Periplus: or, Circumnavigation (of Africa)*, trans. Al. N. Oikonomidēs (Chicago: Ares, 1995), 21–23.
3. Pliny, *Natural History*, trans. H. Rackham (Cambridge, Mass.: Harvard University Press, 1942), vol. 2, book 5, part 8:45, 251.
4. Pliny, book 5, part 5:38, 247; Tacitus, *Complete Works*, trans. Alfred John Church and William Jackson Brodrib (New York: Modern Library, 1942), 628.
5. Herodotus, *The Histories*, trans. A. D. Godley (London: W. Heinemann, 1924), vol. 2, book IV, 387.
6. "Tribes" in "tribespeople" here refers to maximal descent units (one level above "clan") and not ethnic groups. Its Arabic equivalent, *qabila*, is widely used for both Arabic and Berber-speaking pastoral groups, but it is inappropriate in most sub-Saharan African cases except when referring to contemporary ethnic politics.
7. N. Levtzion and J. F. P. Hopkins, eds., *Corpus of Early Arabic Sources for West African History*, trans. J. F. P. Hopkins (Princeton, N.J.: Markus Wiener, 2000), 12–13.
8. Michael Brett, "Islam and Trade in the Bilad Al-Sudan, Tenth-Eleventh Century A.D.," *Journal of African History* 24 (1983): 433.

CHAPTER 2

1. Charles de la Roncière, *La découverte de l'Afrique au Moyen Age* (Cairo: Société royale de géographie de l'Égypte, 1925), vol. 1, 158 (author's translation).
2. Ibn Fadl Allah al-Umari, "Pathways of Vision," in Levtzion and Hopkins, *Corpus of Early Arabic Sources*, 267.
3. Levtzion and Hopkins, *Corpus of Early Arabic Sources*, 170.
4. John O. Hunwick and Eve Trout Powell, *The African Diaspora in the Mediterranean Lands of Islam* (Princeton, N.J.: Markus Wiener, 2002), 106.
5. Eugene Daumas, *Le grand désert: itinéraire d'une caravane du Sahara au pays des nègres, royaume de Haoussa* (Paris: Quintette, 1985), 59 (author's translation).
6. Ghislaine Lydon, *On Trans-Saharan Trails: Islamic Law, Trade Networks and Cross-cultural Exchange in Western Africa* (New York: Cambridge University Press, 2008), 278.
7. Levtzion and Hopkins, *Corpus of Early Arabic Sources*, 322.
8. James L. A. Webb Jr., *Desert Frontier: Ecological and Economic Change along the Western Sahel, 1600–1850* (Madison: University of Wisconsin Press, 1995), 110.

CHAPTER 3

1. John Hunwick, *Timbuktu and the Songhay Empire: Al-Sa'di's "Ta'rikh Al-Sudan" down to 1613 and other Contemporary Documents* (Leiden: Brill, 1999), 190.
2. Levtzion and Hopkins, *Corpus of Early Arabic Sources*, 109–10.
3. Ibid., 296.
4. Ibid., 262.
5. Ibid.
6. Hunwick, *Timbuktu*, 91.
7. Ibid., 102–3.
8. Muhammad al-Ṣaghīr ibn Muhammad Ifrānī, *Nozhet-elhâdi; histoire de la dynastie saadienne au Maroc (1511–1670)*, ed. and trans. O. Houdas (Paris: E. Leroux, 1888–89), vol. 2, 160 (author's translation).
9. Bintou Sanankoua, *Un empire peul au XIXe siècle: la Diina du Maasina* (Paris: Karthala, 1990), 35 (author's translation).
10. Letter of Ahmad ibn Muhammad al-Shinqiti, in *After the Jihad : the Reign of Ahmad Al-Kabir in the Western Sudan*, ed. John Hanson and David Robinson (East Lansing: Michigan State University Press, 1991), 83.
11. Levtzion and Hopkins, *Corpus of Early Arabic Sources*, 188.
12. Dierk Lange, *Le dīwān des sultans du (Kānem-)Bornū: chronologie et histoire d'un royaume africain (de la fin du Xe siècle jusqu'à 1808)* (Wiesbaden: F. Steiner, 1977), 76 (author's translation).
13. Dierk Lange, *A Sudanic Chronicle: The Borno Expeditions of Idris Alauma (1564–1576) According to the Account of Ahmad b. Furtu* (Stuttgart: Steiner, 1987), 35, 70.
14. Gustav Nachtigal, *Sahara und Sudan: Ergebnisse sechsjähriger Reisen in Afrika* (Berlin: Weidmann, 1879), vol. 1, 592 (author's translation).
15. David Robinson and Douglas Smith, *Sources of the African Past: Case Studies of Five Nineteenth-Century African Societies* (New York: Africana, 1979), 140–42; Mervyn Hiskett, *The Sword of Truth; The Life and Times of the Shehu Usuman dan Fodio* (New York: Oxford University Press, 1973), 77.
16. Lange, *Sudanic Chronicle*, 38.
17. Robinson and Smith, *Sources of the African Past*, 136–37.
18. Levtzion and Hopkins, *Corpus of Early Arabic Sources*, 348.
19. A. D. H. Bivar, "Arabic Documents of Northern Nigeria," *Bulletin of the School of Oriental and African Studies* 22 (1959): 339.

CHAPTER 4

1. Levtzion and Hopkins, *Corpus of Early Arabic Sources*, 79–80.
2. Walter J. Skellie, "A Translation of as Sanusi's Creed *Umm Al Barahin*, and a Comparison of It with the Creeds of Al Fadali and an Nasafi." Master's thesis, Hartford Seminary, 1930, 45.
3. Levtzion and Hopkins, *Corpus of Early Arabic Sources*, 296–97.
4. From the twelfth-century biographical dictionary *Tartīb al-madārik* (The Ordering of Comprehensions), by Iyad ibn Musa al-Qadi, http://bewley.virtualave.net/mad1.html.
5. Abu Ubayd Abd Allah al-Bakri, "The Book of Routes and Realms," in Levtzion and Hopkins, *Corpus of Early Arabic Sources*, 72.
6. John O. Hunwick, *Sharia in Songhay: The Replies of al-Maghili to the Questions of Askia al-Hajj Muhammad* (London: Oxford University Press, 1985), 93.

7. Aziz A Batran, *The Qadiryya Brotherhood in West Africa and the Western Sahara: The Life and Times of Shaykh Al-Mukhtar Al-Kunt, (1729–1811)* (Rabat, Morocco: Université Mohammed V, 2001), 163.

8. Sanankoua, *Un empire peul au XIXe siècle*, 58–59 (author's translation).

9. Hiskett, *Sword of Truth*, 66.

10. Hanson and Robinson, *After the Jihad*, 88.

11. Knut S. Vikør, *Sufi and Scholar on the Desert Edge: Muhammad b. Alī al-Sanūsī and His Brotherhood* (Evanston, Ill.: Northwestern University Press, 1995), 202.

12. Thomas C. Hunter, "The Jabi Ta'rikhs: Their Significance in West African Islam," *International Journal of African Historical Studies* 9 (1976): 444.

CHAPTER 5

1. John O. Hunwick, *Jews of a Saharan Oasis: Elimination of the Tamantit Community* (Princeton, N.J.: Markus Wiener, 2006), 13.

2. S. D. Goitein, *A Mediterranean Society: The Jewish Communities of the Arab World as Portrayed in the Documents of the Cairo Geniza* (Berkeley: University of California Press, 1967), vol. 1, *Economic Foundations*, 280–81.

3. Mungo Park, *Travels, in the Interior Districts of Africa: Performed Under the Direction and Patronage, of the African Association, in the Years 1795, 1796, and 1797* (New York: J. Tiebout, 1800), 207.

4. Hunwick, *Timbuktu and the Songhay Empire*, 200.

5. Lange, *Le dīwān des sultans du (Kānem-)Bornū*, 68–69 (author's translation).

6. Mervyn Hiskett, *A History of Hausa Islamic Verse* (London: University of London School of Oriental and African Studies, 1975), 3.

7. Ibn Khaldun, *The Muqaddimah: An Introduction to History*, trans. Franz Rosenzweig (New York: Pantheon, 1958), vol. 3, 420.

8. *The Merchant of Art: An Egyptian Hilali Oral Epic Poet in Performance* (Berkeley: University of California Press, 1987), 67.

9. Levtzion and Hopkins, *Corpus of Early Arabic Sources*, 293.

10. Ibid.

11. Hiskett, *History of Hausa Islamic Verse*, 29.

12. "The Path of Truth," in *Collected Works of Nana Asma'u, Daughter of Usman dan Fodiyo (1793–1864)*, ed. and trans. Jean Boyd and Beverly Mack (East Lansing: Michigan State University Press, 1997), 179.

13. Tierno Mouhammadou-Samba Mombéyâ, *Le filon du bonheur éternel*, ed. and trans. Alfâ Ibrâhîm Sow (Paris: A. Colin, 1971), 43 (author's translation).

14. Christiane Seydou, *Bergers des mots: poésie peule du Mâssina* (Paris: Les Belles Lettres, 1991), 291 (author's translation).

15. Lilyan Kesteloot and Bassirou Dieng, *Les épopées d'Afrique noire* (Paris: Karthala, 1997), 349.

16. Christiane Seydou, *Silâmaka et Poullôri: récit épique peul* (Paris: A. Colin, 1972), 42 (author's translation).

CHAPTER 6

1. Dixon Denham and Hugh Clapperton. *Narrative of Travels and Discoveries in Northern and Central Africa, in the Years 1822, 1823, and 1824* (London: John Murray, 1826), part 2, 92–93.

2. Adolphe Duponchel, *Le chemin de fer Trans-Saharien, jonction coloniale entre l'Algérie et le Soudan: études préliminaires du projet et rapport de mission* (Paris: Hachette, 1879), 28 (author's translation).

3. Douglas Porch, *The Conquest of the Sahara* (New York: Knopf, 1984), 127.

4. Fernand Foureau, *D'Alger au Congo par le Tchad: mission saharienne Foureau-Lamy* (Paris: Masson, 1902), 797–98 (author's translation).

5. Ibid., 798.

6. Ahmadou Kourouma, *The Suns of Independence*, trans. Adrian Adams (New York: Africana, 1981), 13.

7. Jean Tilho, "Variations et disparition possible du Tchad," *Annales de Géographie* 37 (1928): 258 (author's translation).

8. Richard Roberts, *Two Worlds of Cotton: Colonialism and the Regional Economy in the French Soudan, 1800–1946* (Stanford, Calif.: Stanford University Press, 1996, 122.

9. A. H. M. Kirk-Greene, *The Principles of Native Administration in Nigeria: Selected Documents, 1900–1947* (London: Oxford University Press, 1965), 43, 68.

10. Amadou Hampâté Bâ, *Oui mon commandant!: mémoires (II)* (Arles: Actes Sud. 1994), 352 (author's translation).

11. Raphael Danziger, *Abd al-Qadir and the Algerians: Resistance to the French and Internal Consolidation* (New York: Holmes & Meier, 1977), 79.

12. Jamil M. Abun-Nasr, *The Tijaniyya, a Sufi Order in the Modern World* (London: Oxford University Press, 1965), 69 (author's translation).

13. Jean-Louis Triaud, *La légende noire de la Sanûsiyya: une confrérie musulmane saharienne sous le regard français (1840–1930)* (Paris: Maison des sciences de l'homme, 1995), vol. 1, 334 (author's translation).

14. Jean-Louis Triaud, *Tchad 1900–1902, une guerre franco-libyenne oubliée?: une confrérie musulmane, la Sanûsiyya face à la France* (Paris: L'Harmattan, 1987), 33 (author's translation).

15. Kirk-Greene, *Principles of Native Administration*, 43.

16. Christopher Harrison and Paul Marty, *France and Islam in West Africa, 1860–1960* (Cambridge: Cambridge University Press, 1988), 116.

17. Ibid., 166.

18. Sylvianne Garcia, "Al-Hajj Seydou Nourou Tall, grand marabout tijani: l'histoire d'une carrière," in *Le temps des marabouts: itinéraires et stratégies islamiques en Afrique occidentale française v. 1880–1960*, ed. David Robinson et Jean-Louis Triaud (Paris: Karthala, 1997), 254–55 (author's translation).

19. Serge Jouin et al. *L'école en Algérie, 1830–1962: de la régence aux centres sociaux éducatifs* (Paris: Association "Les amis de Max Marchand, de Mouloud Ferdoun et de leurs compagnons," 2001), 31–32 (author's translation).

20. R. M. East, "A First Essay in Imaginative African Literature," *Africa: Journal of the International African Institute* 9 (1936): 352.

21. Robin Leonard Bidwell, *Morocco under Colonial Rule: French Administration of Tribal Areas 1912–1956* (London: Cass, 1973), 52–53 (author's translation).

22. Joseph Luccioni, "L'élaboration du Dahir berbère du 16 Mai 1930," *Revue de l'occident musulman et de la mediterannée* 38 (1984): 73 (author's translation).

23. Gilbert Vieillard, "Poèmes Peuls de Fouta Djallon," *Bulletin du Comité d'études historiques et scientifiques de l'Afrique occidentale française* 20 (1937): 249 (author's translation).

24. Ali Merad, *Le réformisme musulman en Algérie de 1925 à 1940: essai d'histoire religieuse et sociale* (Paris: Mouton, 1967), 416 (author's translations).

25. James McDougall, *History and the Culture of Nationalism in Algeria* (Cambridge: Cambridge University Press, 2006), 133.

26. Merad, 392, 397–98 (author's translations).

27. Marcel Cardaire, *L'Islam et le terroir africain: études soudaniennes* (Koulouba, [Mali]: Impr. du Gouvernement, 1954), 97 (author's translation).

Further Reading

GENERAL HISTORIES

Abun-Nasr, Jamil M. *A History of the Maghrib*. Cambridge: Cambridge University Press, 1975.

Ajayi, J. F. Ade, and Michael Crowder, eds. *History of West Africa*. 2 vols. New York: Columbia University Press, 1972–76.

Ajayi, J. F. Ade, and Michael Crowder. *Historical Atlas of Africa*. Essex, England: Longman, 1985.

Iliffe, John. *Africans: the History of a Continent*. Cambridge: Cambridge University Press, 1995.

"The Sahara: Past, Present and Future." Special issue, *Journal of North African Studies* 10, 3–4 (September–December 2005).

UNESCO International Scientific Committee for the Drafting of a General History of Africa. *General History of Africa*. 8 vols. London: Heinemann Educational Books, 1981–93.

DOCUMENTS

Farias, P. F. de Moraes. *Arabic Medieval Inscriptions from the Republic of Mali: Epigraphy, Chronicles, and Songhay-Tuareg History*. Oxford: Oxford University Press, 2003.

Hunwick, John. *Timbuktu and the Songhay Empire: Al-Sa'di's "Ta'rikh Al-Sudan" down to 1613 and Other Contemporary Documents*. Leiden: Brill, 1999.

Hunwick, John O., and Eve Trout Powell. *The African Diaspora in the Mediterranean Lands of Islam*. Princeton, N.J.: Markus Wiener, 2002.

Levtzion, Nehemia, and J. F. P. Hopkins. *Corpus of Early Arabic Sources for West African History*. Princeton, N.J.: Markus Wiener, 2000.

PEOPLES, REGIONS, AND STATES

Brett, Michael, and Elizabeth Fentress. *The Berbers*. Oxford: Blackwell, 1996.

Levtzion, Nehemiah. *Ancient Ghana and Mali*. London: Methuen, 1973.

PRE-ISLAMIC HISTORY

De Villiers, Marq, and Sheila Hirtle. *Sahara: A Natural History*. New York: Walker, 2002.

Raven, Susan. *Rome in Africa*. London: Routledge, 1993.

Savage, Elizabeth. *A Gateway to Hell, a Gateway to Paradise: The North African Response to the Arab Conquest*. Princeton, N.J.: Darwin Press, 1997.

ECONOMIC HISTORY AND TECHNOLOGY

Austen, Ralph. *African Economic History: Internal Development and External Dependency*. London: James Currey, 1987.

Bulliet, Richard. *The Camel and the Wheel*. Cambridge: Harvard University Press, 1975.

Hogendorn, Jan, and Marion Johnson. *The Shell Money of the Slave Trade*. Cambridge: Cambridge University Press, 1986.

Law, Robin. *The Horse in West African History: The Role of the Horse in the Societies of Pre-colonial West Africa*. Oxford: Oxford University Press, 1980.

Savage, Elizabeth, ed. *The Human Commodity: Perspectives on the Trans-Saharan Slave Trade*. London: Cass, 1992.

ISLAM

Gibb, H. A. R., et al. *The Encyclopaedia of Islam*. Leiden: Brill, 1960–. Available online at http://brillonline.nl/.

Levtzion, Nehemia, and Randall L. Pouwels, eds. *The History of Islam in Africa*. Athens: Ohio University Press, 2000.

Rippin, Andrew. *Muslims: Their Religious Beliefs and Practices*. London: Routledge, 2001.

Robinson, David. *Muslim Societies in African History*. Cambridge: Cambridge University Press, 2004.

ISLAMICATE CULTURE

Austen, Ralph A., ed. *In Search of Sunjata: The Mande Epic as History, Literature and Performance*. Bloomington: Indiana University Press, 1999.

Boyd, Jean, and Beverly Mack. *One Woman's Jihad: Nana Asma'u, Scholar and Scribe*. Bloomington: Indiana University Press, 2000.

Charry, Eric S. *Mande Music: Traditional and Modern Music of the Maninka and Mandinka of Western Africa*. Chicago: University of Chicago Press, 2000.

Hiskett, Mervyn. *A History of Hausa Islamic Verse*. London: University of London School of Oriental and African Studies, 1975.

Hodgson, Marshall G. S. *The Venture of Islam: Conscience and History in a World Civilization*. Chicago: University of Chicago Press, 1974.

Johnson, John William, Thomas A. Hale, and Stephen Belcher. *Oral Epics from Africa: Vibrant Voices from a Vast Continent*. Bloomington: Indiana University Press, 1997.

Prussin, Labelle. *Hatumere: Islamic Design in West Africa*. Berkeley: University of California Press, 1986.

COLONIALISM AND AFTER

Gérard, Albert S. *African Language Literatures: An Introduction to the Literary History of Sub-Saharan Africa*. Washington, D.C.: Three Continents Press, 1981.

Oliver, Roland, and Anthony Atmore. *Africa since 1800*. Cambridge: Cambridge University Press, 2005.

Porch, Douglas. *The Conquest of the Sahara*. New York: Knopf, 1984.

Ruedy, John. *Modern Algeria: the Origins and Development of a Nation*. Bloomington: Indiana University Press, 2nd ed., 2005.

Websites

Africa Maps Map Collection, Perry-Castañeda Library, University of Texas
www.lib.utexas.edu/maps/africa.html
New and old maps covering all of Africa, available for download as PDFs.

Africa Research Central
www.africa-research.org/
Database of all institutions holding primary sources for African studies. Search by country, type of institution, or type of source.

Africa South of the Sahara: Selected Internet Resources
http://library.stanford.edu/depts/ssrg/africa/
Comprehensive directory of Internet resources from the Stanford University Library Africa Collection. Does not include the Maghrib.

African Studies Internet Resources
www.columbia.edu/cu/lweb/indiv/africa/cuvl/
Divided by topic, scholarly organization, and region, this list of resources from Columbia University Libraries is an excellent starting place for research on the entire continent of Africa.

Herskovits Library of African Studies
www.library.northwestern.edu/africana/
The website of the Melville J. Herskovits Library of African Studies, Northwestern University, which holds the premier collection of information on Africa in the United States. Includes catalogs, databases, and digital collections of maps, photographs, posters, videos, and archival materials.

Libraries of Timbuktu for the Preservation and Promotion of African Literary Heritage
www.sum.uio.no/timbuktu/
Wide range of images, archive information, bibliographies, and links on Arabic manuscripts.

Mande Studies Association (MANSA)
www.txstate.edu/anthropology/mansa/
Photographs, maps, and links on Sudanic Africa.

National Museum of African Art
http://africa.si.edu/collections/index.html
African art from the whole continent in virtual exhibitions, searchable collection and digitized photography archive. Radio Africa streaming.

Saharan Studies Association
http://ssa.asu.edu/
News on research on the Sahara in the arts, humanities, social sciences, and natural sciences.

World Wide Web Library of African Archaeology
www.african-archaeology.net/index.html
    Portal to extensive web resources on African archaeology, including practical guides, field notes, maps, databases, journals, social networks, and institutions.

Writing Berber Languages: A Quick Summary
http://web.archive.org/web/20041205195808/www.geocities.com/lameens/tifinagh/index.html
    Article covering the history, orthography, and practical usage of Berber languages.

Acknowledgments

A lthough some of the pages of this work are based on original research, they are mainly a synthesis of scholarship by others, only some of whom are cited in the notes and the list of further reading. For this effort, I must first acknowledge the excellent collections and ever-helpful staff of two great institutions, the Joseph Regenstein Library at the University of Chicago and the Melville J. Herskovits Library of African Studies at Northwestern University. My access to these resources and the production of the visual materials in this book owes much to my research assistant, Kelly King-O'Brien. I am also indebted to the staff of Networking Services and Information Technologies at the University of Chicago for help with maps and illustrations. Among the many colleagues who have provided assistance and advice (but, of course, bear no responsibility for the results) I especially thank Louis Brenner, Paulo de Moraes Farias, John Hunwick, Ghislaine Lydon, Ann McDougall, Labelle Prussin, Gregg Reynolds (along with other lunchtime denizens of the Chicago Center for Middle Eastern Studies), David Robinson, Susan Slyomovics, Jean-Louis Triaud, John Woods, and the entire membership of MANSA (the Mande Studies Association).

Index

Page numbers in **bold** indicate illustrations.

Askia Muhammad Ture (Songhai), 57, 87–88
Association of Muslim Algerian Ulama (AUMA), 137
Jews as, 100
Awdaghust, 55, 56, 74

al-Baghdadi, Mahmud, 90
Bambara, 42, 58, 107, 136
Bambuk (gold source), 30, 41
banco masonry, 115
Bantu languages, 9
baraka, 89
bards, 56, 102–4, 109, 110, 113. *See also* griots
batin, 95, 96, 97
Bedouin, 38, 39, 90, 104
Bello, Muhammad, 66, 67, 77, 118
death of, 92–93
map drawn by, 67, **68**
Ben Badis, Abdelhamid, 137
Benin, 41
Berbers, 8–9, 11, 13, 18, 86, 101, 106
acquiring camels, 13, 17
Arabic imposed on, 54
Islamic impact on, 19–22, 106
language, 18, 101–2, 105–6
Berlin Congo Conference, 119, 122
Bida, myth of, 41–42
Bight of Biafra, 44
Bilma, 38
Birni Ngazargamo, 44, 63
Borno, 26, 62–63, 64
taxation in, 74
warrior, **72**
brass, 41
British colonialism, xi, 119
indirect rule, 127
rivalry with France, 123–24
schools and religious, cultural policies, 133–34
Buré (gold source), 30, 42
Byzantines, 15, 18, 19, 20, 21

Cairo, 23, 26
camels, 16–17, 35, 36
Berbers acquiring, 17
domestication of, 19
caravan trade, 15–17, 35–39
carbuncles, 15
carnelian, 15
cassava, 45
Catalan Atlas (1375 CE), 23, **24–25**
cattle hides, 40, 41, 100, 125
cereal grains, 40
chariot routes, 12
Charles X (French king), 122
Cheggueun (caravan guide), 37
Christianity, 18, 43
reconquest of Iberia, 99
Islam removing all traces of North African, 99
missionaries, 131
climate, 6
of Egypt, 4
of Ghana, 55
of Mediterranean, 4
of Nubia, 4
compass, 36, 38
copper, 40, 41
cotton, 40, 125
Coulibaly dynasty (Segu), 58
Biton Coulibaly, 58–59
cowrie shell currency, 46, 48–47
Cresques, Abraham, **24–25**, 100
Cyrenaica, 10, 94, 130, 131

Dar Tichett, 5
dates, 40
dhimmis, 99
Dhu al-Qarnayn (Alexander the Great), 98
Diwan [Chronicle] of [Kanem-] Borno, 102–3
Donatists, 18
donkeys, 12
drought, 42, 55, 125

Dyula, 107, 136. *See also* Juula
   merchants

Écoles Franco-Berberes, 134–35
Egypt, 5, 10
   camels appearing in, 17
   climate of, 4
   gold trade, 15
   Islam expanding into, 19
   Nubia, trade with, 5, 11–12
   Ottoman conquest of, 71
Elmina Castle, 44
epics, 104, 121
   Arabic, 104, **105**
   Fulani, 111, 113–14
   Mande, 109, **110**, 111
"Ethiopian" (Greek term), 8, 16
Europe
   competing in gold trade, 27
   export goods sought by, 43
   gold trade advantage of, 44
   industrial revolution in, 119
   interfering with slave trade, 124
   Islam resistance to rule by, 128, 130
   motivations for colonizing Africa,
      122
European explorers and colonial
     figures
   Belime, Ernest, 126
   Cardaire, Marcel, 137
   Clapperton, Hugh, **68**, 118, 119
   Destenave, Georges-Mathieu, 131
   Duponchel, Adolphe, 123
   Duveyrier, Henri, 131
   East, Rupert, 134
   Flatters, Paul, 124
   Fourneau, Fernand, 123, 124
   Lenfant, Eugene, 125
   Lugard, Lord Frederick, 127, 131,
     135
   Lyautey, Marechal Hubert,
     135, **135**
   Malafante, Antonio, 27
   Marty, Paul, 132

Nachtigal, Gustav, 64
Park, Mungo, 100
Salisbury, Lord, 123
Tilho, Jean, 125

Fatimid Caliphate, 84–85
Fazzan desert, 13
Fez, 26, 84
fish, 16, 40
fogarra irrigation, 13
French colonialism, xi, 134–36
   Algeria, 119, 122, 128
   attempt to remedy drought, 125
   relations with African rulers,
     127, 130
   rivalry with Britain, 122–23
Fulani, 9, 60, 111, 114
   language (Fulfulde), 9, 107
   literature, 111–14
   role in jihads, 59ff., 91 ff.
Futa Jallon, 60, 62, 93, 111, 112,
     113, 136

Gao, 26, 42, 57
Garamantes, 13–14, 15, 17
Germa, **14**
Germany, 122
Ghana empire, 39, 41, 55
   al-Bakri on, 78
   collapse of, 41, 55, 86
   as pagan, 86–87
Gibraltar, 21
goatskins, 27, 33, 41, 46, 125
Gobir, 64, 66, 73. *See also*
    Hausa people
gold trade, 27, 30, 43–44, 45
   Akan, *45*
   Arabic accounts of, 30–31
   coinage systems and, 30
   Egypt and, 15
   Europeans in, 27, 44
   Moroccan, 44
   Sudan, 15
   Volta River basin, 42, 43–44

griots, 109, 111. *See also* bards
gum arabic, 43, 47
gypsies, 108

habus. *See* waqf
Hadith, 79–80
hajj. *See* pilgrimage
Hamdullahi (Masina capital), 61, 62,
    91–92
Hampâté Bâ, Amadou, 127–28
Hassani Arabs (Mauritania), 81,
    104, 108
Hausa
    city states, 64–67
    language, 9, 107
    literature, 103, 134
    merchants, 42–43
Herodotus, 1, 13, 16
Hilali (Arab tribe), 54, 104, 106
horses, 12, 18. *See also* wheeled
    vehicles
    value of, 32
    in warfare, 70–71, **72**

Ibadis, 21–22, 84
Ibn Yasin, Abdullah (Almoravids),
    55, 86
Idris Alauma (Borno), 63–64, 71
Ife, 41
indigo dye, 40
inesleman, 80–81
iron working and trade, 8, 10, 46,
    116
Islam, xi, 43. *See also* Shiism; Sufism;
    Sunnism
    boundaries of, 38
    business transparency and, 39
    calendar, 19
    under colonial rule, 128–33
    decoration of objects of, 117
    expansion of, 19–20
    five pillars of, 79
    hidden meanings in, 96
    identified with time/place, 78–79

    impact on Berbers, 106
    origin of, 19
    relationship to state, 80
    reconciling mysticism and
        orthodoxy, 88
    reformist, 137
    sects, 82
    testimony of (Shahadah), 78–79
Islamic law, 43, 69
    commerce and, 22
    contractual agreements and, 38–39
    slavery and, 31, 32
    on wealth seized in warfare, 74
Islamic scholarship, 43, 76, 80
ivory, 33, 43, 48

Jabi Jahanke, 96
Jenne (city), 10, 44, 58
Jews, 99–100, 108
Jibril ibn Umar al-Aqdasi, 92
jihad, 32, 66, 91, 92, 93, 127, 130
    common elements of, 59
    first round of, 59–60
    justification for, 69
Juula merchants, 42, 43, 44, 107,
    95, 125

Kaarta (state), 61, 62
Kanem-Borno empire, 39, 102–3
Kanem empire, 22, 26, 62–63
al-Kanemi, Muhammad al-Amin,
    64, **65**
Kano (city), 26, 44
"Kano Chronicle," 103
Kanuri, 9, 62–63, 103, 105, 107
Katsina (city state), 26, 64
Kawar, 20, 22
Keita dynasty (Mali), 56
Khalwatiyya (Sufi order), 90, 92
Kharijism (Islamic sect), 21–22, 82,
    84
kola nuts, 40, 42
kora (musical instrument), 109, *110*
Kourouma, Ahmadou, 125

Kumbi Saleh (Mauritania), 55
Kunta sheikhs, 90, 91–92, 94

languages and literatures, 105 ff.
　Arabic, 104, 105. *See also* Arabic
　　language
　Fulani, 58–59, 111, 113–14
　Libyan, 18
　Mande, 98, 109, **110**, 111
leather, 40–41, 70, 125
leather workers, 100, 108, 117
Lobbo, Amadu (Masina), 60–61,
　91

madrasa, 88
on Jews, 99
Maghrib (North Africa minus Egypt)
　Barbary corsairs and, 70, 119
　colonization by Arabs, 19f.
　colonization by Phoenicians,
　　Greeks, Romans, 10f.
　colonization by Byzantines,
　　Vandals, 18–19
　ethnic and sectarian divisions, 21
　navigators from, 11
　Phoenician alphabet in, 18
　political divisions in Islamic era, 54
Mahmudiyya (Sufi order), 9
maize, 45
Mali empire, 56–57. *See also* Mansa
　Musa, Sunjata
Malikism, 84, 86, 95, 112–13
　vs. Mutazalism, 82
Malinke, 42, 107, 136
Mande languages and culture,
　107–11
　N'Ko writing system, 136
　nyama, 98
　nyamakalaw, 108, 117
manioc, 45
Mansa Musa
　in Catalan Atlas, 23, **24–25**
　mosques built by, 87, 114–15, **116**
　pilgrimage of, 23, 40, 87

as source of economic
　(mis)information, 30, 56
al-Mansur al Dhahabi, Ahmad
　(Morocco), 44, 58
marabouts, 80–81, 89
Marrakesh (Morocco), 26
Masina empire, 58, 60–61, 67,
　91–92, 113
masks, wooden, 116
Mauritania, 39, 47
Mazata (Berbers), 22
Mecca, 19, 86. *See also* pilgrimage
　Muhammad's Hijra from, 78–79
　origin of Mande Komo cult in, 108
　al-Sanusi and Sokoto rulers flee to,
　　130
　Umar Tal's appointment as Tijani
　　Caliph at, 93
merchants. *See* gold trade; Hausa;
　Juula merchants
metal smiths, 41, 100, 108, 116
money, 46–47
mosques, **83**, **116**
Muhammad, 19, 78–79
al-Mukhtar al-Kunti, Sidi, 90–91.
　See also Kunta sheikhs
al-Mukhtar, Umar (Libya), 131
Muqaddimah (Ibn Khaldun), 101–2
Murids (Sufi order), 132

Nasir ad-Din (Mauritania), 60
Neolithic economy, 6
Niger-Congo languages, 9, 111
Nuru Tal, Seydu ("Grand
　Marabout"), 132

ostrich feather trade, 33, 35, 100
oxen transport, 6, 12, 16, 35

palmetto palm, 48
paper, 27, 39
peanuts, 45, 48, 125
"Periplus of Hanno the Phoenician," 11
petroleum, 138

The
New
Oxford
World
History

The New Oxford World History
provides a comprehensive, synthetic
treatment of the "new world history"
from chronological, thematic, and
geographical perspectives, allowing
readers to access the world's complex
history from a variety of conceptual,
narrative, and analytical viewpoints
as it fits their interests.

Ralph A. Austen is professor emeritus
of African history at the University
of Chicago. His many publications
cover topics ranging from African
economic history, the Atlantic and
trans-Saharan slave trades, African oral
and written literature as well as film
and comparative colonialisms. He has
been a visiting professor at universities
and research centers in Africa, France,
Germany, and Israel.

The
New
Oxford
World
History

CHRONOLOGICAL VOLUMES
The World from 4000 to 1000 BCE
The World from 1000 BCE to 300/500 CE
The World from 300 to 1000 CE
The World from 1000 to 1500
The World in the Eighteenth Century
The World in the Nineteenth Century
The World in the Twentieth Century

THEMATIC AND TOPICAL VOLUMES
The City: A World History
Democracy: A World History
Empires: A World History
The Family: A World History
Race: A World History
Technology: A World History

GEOGRAPHICAL VOLUMES
Central Asia in World History
China in World History
Japan in World History
Russia in World History
The Silk Road in World History
South Africa in World History
South Asia in World History
Southeast Asia in World History
Trans-Saharan Africa in World History